W9-BTI-017

Becky Thompson

Author of *Hope Unfolding*

Susan K. Pitts

MIDNIGHT
MOM
Devotional

365 Prayers to Put Your
Momma Heart to Rest

WATERBROOK

MIDNIGHT MOM DEVOTIONAL

All Scripture quotations, unless otherwise indicated, are taken from the Holy Bible, New International Version®, NIV®. Copyright © 1973, 1978, 1984, 2011 by Biblica Inc.® Used by permission. All rights reserved worldwide. Scripture quotations marked (CSB) are taken from the Christian Standard Bible®, copyright © 2017 by Holman Bible Publishers. Used by permission. Christian Standard Bible® and CSB® are federally registered trademarks of Holman Bible Publishers. Scripture quotations marked (CEV) are taken from the Contemporary English Version. Copyright © 1991, 1992, 1995 by American Bible Society. Used by permission. Scripture quotations marked (ESV) are taken from the Holy Bible, English Standard Version, ESV® Text Edition® (2016), copyright © 2001 by Crossway Bibles, a publishing ministry of Good News Publishers. All rights reserved. Scripture quotations marked (NKJV) are taken from the New King James Version®. Copyright © 1982 by Thomas Nelson Inc. Used by permission. All rights reserved.

Hardcover ISBN 978-0-525-65429-2
eBook ISBN 978-0-525-65430-8

Copyright © 2020 by Rebecca F. Thompson and Susan K. Pitts

Cover design by Mark D. Ford and Becky Thompson

Authors are represented by Alive Literary Agency, www.aliveliterary.com.

All rights reserved. No part of this book may be reproduced or transmitted in any form or by any means, electronic or mechanical, including photocopying and recording, or by any information storage and retrieval system, without permission in writing from the publisher.

Published in the United States by WaterBrook, an imprint of Random House, a division of Penguin Random House LLC.

WATERBROOK® and its deer colophon are registered trademarks of Penguin Random House LLC.

Library of Congress Cataloging-in-Publication Data
Names: Thompson, Becky (Rebecca F.), author. | Pitts, Susan K., 1956– author.
Title: Midnight mom devotional : 365 prayers to put your momma heart to rest / Becky Thompson, Susan K. Pitts.
Description: Colorado Springs : WaterBrook, 2020.
Identifiers: LCCN 2019030059 | ISBN 9780525654292 (hardcover) | ISBN 9780525654308 (ebook)
Subjects: LCSH: Mothers—Prayers and devotions. | Motherhood—Religious aspects—Christianity.
Classification: LCC BV283.M7 T46 2020 | DDC 242/.6431—dc23
LC record available at https://lccn.loc.gov/2019030059

Printed in the United States of America
2020—First Edition

10 9 8 7 6 5 4 3 2

SPECIAL SALES
Most WaterBrook books are available at special quantity discounts when purchased in bulk by corporations, organizations, and special-interest groups. Custom imprinting or excerpting can also be done to fit special needs. For information, please email specialmarketscms@penguinrandom house.com.

From Becky

For my mom, Susan Pitts, who carried on the
generational legacy of praying women and taught
me the power of connecting with the heart of God.
Thank you for always being a praying momma and
teaching me how to be a praying momma too.

From Susan

For my husband, Marc, who has been my
best friend for forty years. Thank you for
your support and belief in this book.
For my Irish grandmother, Catherine Powers,
who was my first example of daily fervent prayer.
For my aunt Mary Benevides, my aunt Rose Ramos,
and Mary DeCosta, who taught me about a
personal relationship with the Lord that included
daily conversations with Him.
Thank you all for teaching me so well.

I dare you to pray life-changing prayers. Ask for heaven to come interrupt every facet of your life. Ask for encounters that ruin you for the mundane and ordinary. Ask for signs, wonders, and supernatural kisses from God daily that cause you to see through the lens of the realm you have access to. Ask for miracles and potent displays of power that pull you out of settling for cheap talk and inspiration. Ask for rain in the dry places of your heart and life, and watch it come. Ask for fresh rivers to flow out of the inside of you. Ask to dream again, but dreams that challenge you and pull you into your destiny. Ask for the nations because they are already yours! Call down fire upon the altar of your home, and see legacy change. Speak breakthrough over immovable and impossible situations. Prophesy restoration, recompense, and restitution. Command sickness to leave, affliction to cease, and bodies and minds to be whole. Pray when you don't feel like it, when it's a sacrifice, when it's worship in the middle of the storm, and watch as God flips the script on every powerless circumstance you lay your eyes upon.

—NATE JOHNSTON, nateandchristy.co

To You, Momma, Before We Begin

Hi, Momma,

We are so glad you have found your way to these words. We have been thinking about you and praying for you, and we believe it is no coincidence that you are reading this book at this exact moment. Let us take just a second to introduce ourselves before we say anything else.

We are Becky Thompson and Susan Pitts.

I (Becky) am Susan's daughter. I began an online ministry for moms back in 2013, speaking mostly about the Father's love for a momma's heart and how He meets us right where we are in our mothering, marriages, and everyday lives. I have written five books in five years, and I host a weekly motherhood podcast, *Revived Motherhood*. I have three kids, Kolton, Kadence, and Jaxton, and I've been married to my husband, Jared, for thirteen years. We live just outside Nashville, but we are Okies at heart.

And I (Susan) am Becky's momma, and I've been in ministry for over forty years in various capacities, including full time, part time, and as a pastor's wife. I moved from the shores of New England to Oklahoma to attend Oral Roberts University. While in

Tulsa, I met and married my husband, Marc Pitts, a graduate of the University of Tulsa College of Law. We have two grown daughters, Beth and Becky, and three grandchildren. Marc and I have ministered faithfully in cities and towns across Oklahoma, serving in established churches, planting churches, and helping launch dozens of new ministries. My heart for families and especially for women's ministries has always been to heal the brokenhearted and to restore women's relationships with the Lord.

So, when did Becky and I start ministering to women together? I suppose it began back when Becky was born. The day I went into labor, Marc was out of town at a job interview in Washington, DC. A neighbor drove me to Mercy Hospital in Oklahoma City, and that's where she was born. I remember feeling very alone and scared even though I knew that Jesus was with me. Mercy Hospital sits on a hill and has a large white cross that is lit up at night to remind everyone that the Lord is with all the patients.

When I went home later that week, I remember sitting in the rocking chair in the midnight hours and seeing that white cross from miles away as a light in the darkness. As I held baby Becky, I thought of the mommas who were having babies and who might also be feeling alone and scared, and I prayed for them. That was when the Midnight Mom prayer time started for me.

Thirty years later, I (Becky) was often awake in the middle of the night with my own baby. My youngest, Jaxton, did not sleep well, and I would find myself up at all hours of the night. Like many moms in my generation, I'd pull out my phone and scroll through social media as I rocked my little baby. One night, I decided to post on my Facebook page a simple message: "Mommas, who is awake tonight and why? Leave your #MidnightMomCheckin in the comments." Women who followed my online ministry commented and said why they were awake, what time it was where they lived, and what was going on around them.

And the Midnight Mom Check-In was born. Hundreds of moms would comment nightly. We heard from women who were awake with their newborns, up with sick children, in the hospital waiting for test results, sleepless because of worry, enjoying the stillness of their houses while everyone else slept, monitoring fevers, changing wet sheets, waiting to hear from children traveling home, anxious about the next day, and going through so many other common motherhood experiences.

Something beautiful happened as we read one another's stories: we began encouraging one another, praying for one another, and helping other mommas know that they are far less alone than they feel in those nighttime hours. The truth is, every night there are mommas across the world who are awake and doing the very same things, and there is a God who wants to meet us in the quiet.

As the Midnight Mom Check-In grew, we needed a place just for these nightly gatherings. So the Midnight Mom Devotional Facebook page was founded. But I couldn't manage it alone. Knowing I needed help encouraging the hundreds of women who would gather each night and share their prayer requests, I invited my mom to pray and post with me. And so what began with a momma and her newborn baby looking out toward a white cross, praying for mommas in the middle of the night, came full circle as nightly this mother-daughter duo began praying for mommas awake around the world.

Many nights, hundreds of prayer requests would pour in for a variety of situations, and we'd pray for all of them. But eventually, we began targeting our nightly momma check-ins toward mommas facing specific situations. And our signature "Tonight we pray for the momma who . . ." prayers began.

Today, just four years after that first group of mommas gathered together online to encourage one another in the midnight hours, we reach over a million mommas nightly.

So, as you pick up this book and read each day, our hope is that you immediately sense the multitude of women all across the world who are praying this prayer on this night with you. Many of these prayers will seem as if they were written just for you and your specific circumstances. They will feel as though God knew exactly what you were experiencing on that particular day and gathered thousands of women to lift you up. On those nights, remember that the Lord knows just what we need to hear and when we need to hear it. You aren't alone, because thousands of other women are praying with you and for you, Momma.

As you go throughout the year, other prayers will seem to fit the lives of women you know—perhaps a momma friend who is a teacher or who has a child with complex medical issues. You might come to a prayer that is for the momma who is moving or the momma who has friends moving away. You might read a prayer for the widowed momma or the military momma or the momma who is getting her degree.

At the end of each night's prayer, we have included a line for you to write the name of the momma you're praying for on that particular night. Our hope is that this book becomes a treasured keepsake as you document the women God has placed on your heart to pray for throughout the year.

If you find that a prayer speaks specifically to what someone else is facing, don't hesitate to take a picture of the prayer and text it or message it to the momma who needs it. Just make sure you tell her where the encouragement came from so she can find the rest of the prayers. They might meet her right where she is too.

Finally, if you are facing a specific situation, we have included a topical index in the back. So, whether you're a single momma, a working momma, an anxious momma, a momma of a child with special needs, or a momma in just about any other situation, we believe you will find a prayer that speaks hope into your unique set of circumstances.

Truly, we are so glad you are joining our community of praying mommas. Your prayers are powerful. They are important. And we are honored to walk each day with you, trusting that the Lord is the one leading us all. Before you begin and jump to today's date, let's pray together.

> *Father, tonight we pray for this momma who is a prayer warrior. She might be saying her first momma prayers tonight, or she might have been praying for years. We ask tonight that she would begin to have deeper conversations with You. We ask that You'd teach her to hear Your voice in response. Bless her as she reads a prayer each night, and help her to expand upon it in her own way. Let these prayers be a starting point for her own conversations with You. We believe You will teach her to pray just as You taught Your disciples in the Bible when they asked. Bless her tonight with rest and peace. We ask in Jesus's name. Amen.*

Friend, we'd love to hear from you. Please send us a message and let us know what this book has meant to you or how it has met you right where you are. And don't forget to join us nightly as we continue to pray for mommas online around the world. You can connect with us and the rest of the midnight mommas in our online community by searching Midnight Mom Devotional, or you can find us on the web at midnightmomdevotional.com.

So much love,
Becky and Susan

Tonight we pray for the momma who is ready for a new beginning. She is all set to leave last year behind her and start fresh with new hope, new joy, and new opportunities in this new year. Lord, Your mercies don't need a new year to begin again. Remind her that Your Word says Your mercies are new each morning. Help her remember this powerful truth every time she takes a breath. Bless this year. Walk with her each step of the way. We ask in Jesus's name. Amen.

> The steadfast love of the LORD never ceases;
>> his mercies never come to an end;
> they are new every morning;
>> great is your faithfulness. (Lamentations 3:22–23, ESV)

Tonight I'm praying this for _____.

January 2

*T*onight we pray for the momma who is concerned that her appearance has changed since she had little ones. She used to look and feel young and healthy. Now when she thinks about the way she looks, she feels discouraged because her body has changed. Lord, we know that You created us and that we are wonderfully made. Tonight we ask that You would bless this momma so she will see herself through Your eyes. You see a woman who has carried children—maybe in her body but absolutely in her arms and heart. She is strong and worthy of respect. Remind her that she is a daughter of the Most High God and that she should speak kindly of herself. Bless her tonight, and fill her with fresh confidence. We ask in Jesus's name. Amen.

> The LORD does not see as man sees; for man looks at the outward appearance, but the LORD looks at the heart.
> (1 Samuel 16:7, NKJV)

Tonight I'm praying this for _____.

#MidnightMomDevotional

January 3

*T*onight we pray for the momma who needs a miracle. Lord, she needs Your peace to overcome the chaos in her life and to bring her life and circumstances into order. She needs You to show Yourself strong on her behalf. Lord, she is trying to believe You will intervene, but there are moments when she feels uncertain. Help this momma call out to You like the parent in Mark 9:24 who cried out to Jesus, "Help me overcome my unbelief!" Tonight, Lord, she asks for a miracle of both belief and healing. She reaches out to You with her prayers. We ask for rest tonight as she leaves it all in Your hands. We ask in Jesus's name. Amen.

Tonight I'm praying this for _____.

January 4

Tonight we pray for the momma whose child has special needs. She didn't plan on this when she dreamed of motherhood, and still she loves her child with all her heart. Oftentimes, people act as if she is a saint or someone special because of how she cares for the one she's been given to love. But the truth is, she is simply a momma loving her baby just like any other momma does. Lord, grant her grace as she walks out this journey on this path. Remind her that You walk with her every step of the way. We ask in Jesus's name. Amen.

Tonight I'm praying this for _____.

Tonight we pray for the momma who has a newborn baby. Lord, this is such a precious time, but it is also an exhausting time. She gets just a few quick hours of rest while the baby is sleeping. She feels as though she is in a fog. She may even have older children to care for while she is still so sleep deprived. Lord, this momma is truly the Midnight Mom who is up while the world sleeps. Please bless her tonight and multiply her rest. Let her feel Your presence as she rocks her baby tonight. We bless her in this holy work of motherhood. We ask in Jesus's name. Amen.

Tonight I'm praying this for _____.

Tonight we pray for the anxious momma who just wants to be whole. Lord, she wants the space in her heart that is currently filled with anxiety to be filled with peace and joy and Your goodness. She is trying to find the switch that turns off all this worry and fear. She knows You are able to do abundantly more than all she asks or thinks. Tonight we ask You to show this momma how to be free from fear and worry. Give her friends, family, and professional help who will walk out this journey of wholeness with her. Help her to rest well tonight. We ask in Jesus's name. Amen.

Tonight I'm praying this for _____.

January 7

Tonight we pray for the momma who doesn't stop. She just keeps putting one foot in front of the other and going forward for her family. The road may be difficult, but she is brave, even though she doesn't always feel that way. Lord, when she wakes up in the morning, her first thought is, *What can I do today to make my family's life better?* She is strong and determined, and she has her heart set on You. Bless her tonight, Lord, and give her a good night's rest. May she wake up tomorrow refreshed and ready to keep going. We ask in Jesus's name. Amen.

Tonight I'm praying this for _____.

*T*onight we pray for the momma who wants to know her destiny, her purpose, her reason for being born. Lord, she senses that life has a greater meaning. We thank You that this momma is searching at the start of the new year. She is searching for Your plan for her life. Now, Lord, we ask that You would lead her to the greatest meaning of all: Your free gift of salvation. As Your Word says in Romans 10:9, "If you declare with your mouth, 'Jesus is Lord,' and believe in your heart that God raised him from the dead, you will be saved." Lord, bless this momma as she finds hope in Your plan for her. Give her the friends she needs to help her live out this life of faith. We ask in Jesus's name. Amen.

Tonight I'm praying this for _____.

January 9

*T*onight we pray for the momma whose spouse is in law enforcement. There are many types of law enforcement officers, including the police, sheriff's department, correctional officers, and more. These spouses put themselves in harm's way to protect the community and to provide for the families they love. Lord, first we ask that You would protect them. Let Your angels encamp around them and help them on their shifts. We pray also for peace for this momma's heart as her spouse continues to work in his chosen profession. Bless them both tonight. We ask in Jesus's name. Amen.

Tonight I'm praying this for _____.

Tonight we pray for the momma who is trying to live a healthier life at the start of the year. This is harder than some might think. She may be having cravings. She may be struggling to keep going to the gym. She may want to just give up. But she is doing this so she will be healthier for her children and for herself. She is trying to lead by example in her nutrition and exercise. Bless this momma tonight, and help her be strong in her battle. She can do this because You are giving her the strength to carry on each day. We ask in Jesus's name. Amen.

Tonight I'm praying this for _____.

January 11

Tonight we pray for the momma who needs someone to hold her up. She feels like a weeping willow that is bent over by the weight of its branches. Lord, she needs someone to come alongside her and help her stand tall and not be burdened by the cares of the day. She needs an encouraging friend who will speak truth to her and remind her that it will not always be this way or this hard. Lord, help this momma tonight who feels as if she is collapsing under the weight of it all. Help her rest and awaken tomorrow refreshed with a new strength. We ask in Jesus's name. Amen.

Tonight I'm praying this for _____.

Tonight we pray for the momma who is homeschooling her children. Lord, this is a calling that is all encompassing. Her children have a variety of educational needs, and she is working hard to fill them. There are many curriculum choices and endless opportunities for outside activities to help strengthen her children's learning experience, and it's up to this momma to make the best decisions. Be with this homeschooling momma as she follows Your lead and teaches her children with You as her guide. We ask in Jesus's name. Amen.

Tonight I'm praying this for _____.

January 13

Tonight we pray for the momma who is caring for a sick child. She may have an infant who is miserable with his first cold. Or she may have a toddler with an ear infection. She may have a little one who normally loves to go to school and play games and is always full of life, but tonight, Lord, this little one is running a fever and just feels so sick. Her momma heart is worried. She doesn't like it when her children are not well. Tonight as she sits up in the night hours watching over her child, remind her that they are both covered by the blanket of Your love and healing. Remind her that she is not alone. We ask for healing and rest tonight. We ask in Jesus's name. Amen.

Tonight I'm praying this for _____.

Tonight we pray for the momma who feels as if she is climbing uphill. She feels as though this mountain has no top and she will never reach the summit. Motherhood is so much harder than she imagined. She loves her children, but the constant daily struggle to do everything is wearing on her heart and mind today. Lord, we pray for this momma. We ask that You would remind her that she is never alone. Let her know that we, a community of praying women all over the world, are praying for her tonight in her climb. Please remind her that You are with her every single step of this journey. Give her sweet sleep tonight as she rests and prepares for another day. We ask in Jesus's name. Amen.

Tonight I'm praying this for _____.

*T*onight we pray for the momma who has adopted her child. She loves this child with a fierce momma heart. This love grew with every step she took through the legal system to make this child her own. While waiting for the adoption papers to go through, at times she could hardly breathe because she was so anxious, wondering if it would all work out. But, Lord, You were right there with her every step of the process. You knew all the obstacles she would encounter as she prepared to make this child her own. You saw her through every valley and mountaintop. Bless her tonight with sweet rest. We ask in Jesus's name. Amen.

Tonight I'm praying this for _____.

*T*onight we pray for the momma who feels as if she is at the bottom of her barrel and has nothing left to give. Lord, she feels as if she has run out of joy, out of peace, out of patience, and even out of time to find a way to refill this emptiness deep within her heart. Lord, You give us an abundance of peace, and You teach us patience. You can fully fill this momma's heart again. Lord, we thank You because You give all these things freely to us when we simply ask. Please help this momma ask You for exactly what she needs tonight. Multiply whatever sleep she is able to get so that it is sufficient for tomorrow. We ask in Jesus's name. Amen.

Tonight I'm praying this for _____.

Tonight we pray for the momma who is carrying her fear with her like a heavy backpack full of worry and stress. She knows she needs to put it down. She knows she needs to lay it at the feet of Jesus. She remembers that Jesus said His yoke is easy and His burden light. But she trudged through the day, carrying this heavy load, unable to pause or put it down. Tonight, Lord, we ask You to help her. You are more than able to take care of all the things she worries about daily. We ask that You would help her find rest and peace tonight in the knowledge that tomorrow is a new day. We ask in Jesus's name. Amen.

> Come to me, all you who are weary and burdened, and I will give you rest. Take my yoke upon you and learn from me, for I am gentle and humble in heart, and you will find rest for your souls. For my yoke is easy and my burden is light. (Matthew 11:28–30)

Tonight I'm praying this for _____.

January 18

Tonight we pray for the momma who is sick. Lord, she has a cold or allergies or maybe even the flu. She might have a fever, and her whole body may be hurting. Lord, mommas don't have sick days off. They have to just keep going, no matter how they feel. Tonight we pray that You would heal her from the top of her head to the tips of her toes. Grant her sweet, restorative sleep. Help her feel much better tomorrow morning when she wakes up. Return health to her home. We ask in Jesus's name. Amen.

Tonight I'm praying this for _____.

January 19

Tonight we pray for the momma of teenagers. Lord, this momma is going through a season that is like no other. She is dealing with all the stresses of her children's growing independence, including dating, driving, and education and career goals, as well as all the other complicated situations that arise in a teen's life. Lord, tonight we ask that You would remind her that You are always with her children. You never leave them or forsake them. Even when she is not there or close at hand, You are right next to them. Lord, tonight we ask for peace so she can rest and for hope for tomorrow. We ask in Jesus's name. Amen.

Tonight I'm praying this for _____.

*T*onight we pray for the momma whose family makes it more difficult. Sometimes they can be so supportive, but other times her heart is hurt by the things they say and do. Lord, tonight please heal every wounded place and restore every relationship. Please release her heart from the trauma caused by unsupportive loved ones. Bring her peace in her decisions, knowing that she is a good momma as she seeks Your face and Your wisdom for herself and her children. We ask in Jesus's name. Amen.

Tonight I'm praying this for _____.

#MidnightMomDevotional

January 21

Tonight we pray for the momma with a house full of opinions. Whether she has demanding toddlers or strong-minded teenagers, she is constantly keeping order in the midst of chaos. She is a persistent peacemaker. She calms stressful situations. She points to truth. She listens and helps walk the hearts of those she loves toward what's right and what's real. It's not always easy, Lord. You see how hard it is to guide and direct children with such strong opinions. So, Lord, bring her peace tonight. Strengthen her heart. Give her fresh grace to guide the future leaders You have placed in her care. Help her remember she's not doing it alone. We ask in Jesus's name. Amen.

Tonight I'm praying this for _____.

Tonight we pray for the momma who is in her first trimester of pregnancy. She is still getting used to the idea that she is having a baby. She might be suffering from morning sickness and feeling miserable. Congratulations keep pouring in, and there is excitement as everyone anticipates this baby. Lord, she is dreaming about the new life inside her, but she is also nervous as she considers the future and this little one's health. Tonight, Lord, bless this momma, calm her fears, and help her enjoy this wonderful stage of pregnancy. Help her rest tonight. Bless her and her baby. We ask in Jesus's name. Amen.

Tonight I'm praying this for _____.

January 23

*T*onight we pray for the momma who is single. Some days it feels impossible to accomplish everything that is necessary to make the household run smoothly. Some days she feels as if she drops the ball or her children suffer because she has to fill the role of both parents. Lord, she tries so hard and does her very best. Tonight we pray that You would give her extra wisdom, extra grace, extra strength for the days ahead. Remind her that You walk with her daily. Help her rest tonight so she can start fresh tomorrow. We ask in Jesus's name. Amen.

Tonight I'm praying this for _____.

Tonight we pray for the momma who is experiencing sorrow. Her heart is broken in two. She may even feel as if it is shattered into a million pieces. She has suffered a tremendous loss and has to find a way to move on in this new normal. Lord, this is not an easy task. It feels overwhelming at times. She feels as though she is walking alone. Lord, tonight please remind this momma that You are right there with her. Please remind her that You never leave her or forsake her. Please begin the healing process for this sorrow. Help this momma find the right resources she needs to keep moving forward. Give her a good night's sleep. We ask in Jesus's name. Amen.

Tonight I'm praying this for _____.

Tonight we pray for the momma who is tired. She may still be exhausted from the holidays or be recovering from a winter cold or the flu. She is ready for a routine, for health, and for everything to finally feel settled. Lord, this momma is tired for so many different reasons. She is exhausted to her bones. Help this momma find full healing and restorative rest in You tonight. Give her Your strength for tomorrow. Give her hope for the days ahead. We ask in Jesus's name. Amen.

Tonight I'm praying this for _____.

January 26

*T*onight we pray for the momma whose spouse is deployed overseas. She worries about his safety. He often cannot tell her where he is or what he is doing, but she knows he thinks about her and their children every day. He does this work for his country and also for his family because he wants a safer world to live in. Lord, bless this momma and her spouse tonight. Keep him safe, and help them through the days until his deployment ends. We are so thankful for their service as a family. Give this momma rest tonight. We ask in Jesus's name. Amen.

Tonight I'm praying this for _____.

Tonight we pray for the momma who is struggling to make ends meet. She has more month left at the end of her money than she has money left at the end of her month. She is trying to budget and conserve, but she may face unexpected medical bills, school needs, car repairs, and so much more. She feels as if she can't catch up, never mind get ahead. Lord, You say in Philippians 4:19 that You will supply all our needs according to Your riches in glory. This momma trusts You. You are her provider. We ask for peaceful rest tonight as she sleeps, knowing that You are taking care of tomorrow and any challenge that comes her way. We ask in Jesus's name. Amen.

Tonight I'm praying this for _____.

*T*onight we pray for the momma who is suffering from depression. Lord, it is an illness as real as any physical pain or disease. She carries it with her like a heavy blanket everywhere she goes. Sometimes she feels as though she can't get out from underneath it. Lord, lead this momma out of the hidden places and into the light of Your goodness and grace. Guide her as she seeks every resource she needs. Lead her onto the path to wholeness. Help the body of Christ remove all stigma from this disease so that she may find strength and healing among her fellow believers. We ask in Jesus's name. Amen.

Tonight I'm praying this for _____.

January 29

Tonight we pray for the momma who is trying to find her balance. She may have added a new baby to the family or a new job or a new project, and now the household has shifted. Lord, we know it takes time to adjust to new things and new people. We are so grateful You give us the time we need to get comfortable in each situation so we can find the joy in new things. Bless this momma tonight as she finds her balance and teaches her family how to find theirs. Help her rest well tonight and be ready for the new day tomorrow. We ask in Jesus's name. Amen.

Tonight I'm praying this for _____.

*T*onight we pray for the momma who feels as if she is on top of being a momma. She feels she has it all figured out, right in this moment. She feels she has a handle on the responsibilities and the activities and all the exciting things that make being a momma great. Lord, help her remember this mountaintop moment. Help her cherish this feeling and store it up in her heart. No matter what tomorrow brings, You are right there beside her through each challenge and celebration. Help her rest well tonight. We ask in Jesus's name. Amen.

Tonight I'm praying this for _____.

January 31

*T*onight we pray for the momma who feels as though she is fighting against time. She may have little ones growing up too fast or a high schooler sending off college applications, or her grown child might even be planning a wedding. She wonders, *How did it go so quickly? Where did all the time go?* Tonight, Lord, we ask that You would help this momma take in the beauty of motherhood amid the chaos. Help her breathe in the joy of the everyday journey before it swoops by and is gone in an instant. Bless her tonight. We ask in Jesus's name. Amen.

Tonight I'm praying this for _____.

*T*onight we pray for the momma whose child has heart disease. It can be so traumatic for a momma to receive this diagnosis and then begin the process of walking out this journey. Lord, please be with this momma as she navigates the medical procedures and the care of her precious child. Lord, wrap her and her little one in Your arms of love and protection. Watch over this family. Bring them the answers, resources, and medical team they need. Send friends who will walk this road with them. We ask in Jesus's name. Amen.

Tonight I'm praying this for _____.

#MidnightMomDevotional

February 2

Tonight we pray for the momma who is a foster momma. She has welcomed into her heart and home a child or children who still belong to another. She went through training, special home inspections, and countless other steps to be able to shelter these little ones in great need. We ask, Lord, that You help her as she loves, cares for, and nurtures these children and then continues to trust You with whatever comes next. Help her rest tonight, and fill her home with peace. We ask in Jesus's name. Amen.

Tonight I'm praying this for _____.

*T*onight we pray for the momma who needs the Lord to wash away the day. It was a long one. She is ready for tomorrow to be different. But before she climbs into bed and falls asleep, she just needs everything she's been through to be wiped away. Lord, wash her heart with Your love. Refresh her with Your Spirit. Take away the dust of the day that covers her heart in guilt. Remind her that she is a good mom and that tomorrow will be different. Help her hear the hope found in that. Take her from a place of feeling overwhelmed to a place of peace. Give her rest tonight. We ask in Jesus's name. Amen.

Tonight I'm praying this for _____.

#MidnightMomDevotional

February 4

*T*onight we pray for the momma whose heart is threadbare. In some aspects of her life she feels continually worn down, and in others she feels weak and vulnerable. Lord, come close to this momma with Your healing love. Strengthen and heal the parts of her that need Your touch. You aren't just her healer; You are her comforter. Minister to the areas that only You and she know need mending. Touch her life and strengthen her soul. Thank You for fashioning Your love into a blanket of peace that reinforces each weak place within her. We ask in Jesus's name. Amen.

Tonight I'm praying this for _____.

Tonight we pray for the momma who feels as though she can't catch a rhythm. When she gets caught up, she seems to fall behind in a different area. When she gains ground in one thing, she loses it somewhere else. Lord, this momma is exhausted from trying. She can see just how far she has to go and has no idea how she is going to get it all done. Give this momma a strategy. Give her a practical plan to take on everything she is facing. And in the midst of it all, give her grace for what she is able to accomplish and what she isn't. She is Your beloved daughter. Reveal how much You love her. We ask in Jesus's name. Amen.

Tonight I'm praying this for _____.

February 6

*T*onight we pray for the momma who wants to develop her own prayer time with You, Lord. We ask that this momma would begin to have deeper conversations with You. We ask that You'd teach her to hear Your voice in response. Bless her nightly as she reads each prayer, and help her expand upon it in her own way. Let these prayers be a starting point for her own. We believe You will teach her to pray just as You taught Your disciples in the Bible when they asked. Bless her tonight with rest and peace. We ask in Jesus's name. Amen.

> One day Jesus was praying in a certain place. When he finished, one of his disciples said to him, "Lord, teach us to pray, just as John taught his disciples." (Luke 11:1)

Tonight I'm praying this for _____.

Tonight we pray for the momma who is up late with her sick child. Despite her weariness, she is more concerned with her little one who may have a fever, congestion, or an upset tummy than she is about getting sleep. Some nights, teething brings on earaches, and some nights are filled with croup and breathing treatments. Lord, please be with this momma right now. Remind her that she is not alone and that the Great Physician is keeping watch with her. We ask for Your healing touch for her child. We ask in Jesus's name. Amen.

Tonight I'm praying this for _____.

February 8

Tonight we pray for the momma who is afraid of what the world is becoming. She hears so many terrible stories on the news and social media. Everything just seems to be much worse than it was when she was little. She worries about her children and the future they will live in. Lord, remind this momma that You created this world and that You have a divine plan for Your creation. Remind her that she can trust in You for things that are too big to handle on her own. Bring her peace and rest. We ask in Jesus's name. Amen.

Tonight I'm praying this for _____.

Tonight we pray for the momma who is a pastor's wife and feels she is raising her children in a fishbowl. Everyone can see everything and has an opinion, which creates some unique parenting challenges. Lord, please help her balance the responsibilities she has for the congregation, the community, and her children—not necessarily in that order. Resolve any issues that have arisen from being both a pastor's wife and a momma. Bless her tonight with peace. We ask in Jesus's name. Amen.

Tonight I'm praying this for _____.

Tonight we pray for the momma who stands outside the circle and just looks in. She feels shut out of so many things that matter to her. Sometimes she feels excluded from her family, her group of friends, maybe even her church. Lord, tonight we pray for this momma who needs to feel included. Lord, You are the one who makes the way. You are the one who opens doors. Tonight we ask that You would open the right doors for this momma so that those around her welcome her in. Give her sweet sleep tonight. We ask in Jesus's name. Amen.

Tonight I'm praying this for _____.

Tonight we pray for the momma who is entering into a new relationship. Lord, for whatever reason, she has found herself alone and without a companion to walk with on this journey. Lord, she believes You have opened the door to this new relationship. We pray tonight that You give her wisdom and discernment. We pray for wise counsel from those she knows and trusts to give her sound guidance in this area. You care about her heart and will help her navigate the steps ahead. Give her rest tonight. We ask in Jesus's name. Amen.

Tonight I'm praying this for _____.

*T*onight we pray for the momma who would love to find a moment to sit down. She is always going. She is always moving from one need to the next. She continually looks toward the future. Lord, help this momma find a moment to rest. Help her find five minutes to just pause and center her heart on Your truth. You are so proud of her. You see the work she does for her family. You see how she just keeps going. And, Lord, You don't want her to burn out. Meet this momma in a moment of rest. We ask in Jesus's name. Amen.

Tonight I'm praying this for _____.

February 13

*T*onight we pray for the momma who needs to know where You were. She has walked some hard roads. She has been through so much. And some days You have felt far away. Lord, show this momma that each tear she cried You cried too. Show her that You took each hard step with her. Reveal exactly how You held her when her heart was breaking. Speak peace over her now as she realizes she was never actually alone. You were with her. You *are* with her. Help her learn to trust You even more fully. Help her look for You in the hard moments ahead. Give her confidence that You are a good God and she can follow You. Please bless her with sleep tonight. We ask in Jesus's name. Amen.

Tonight I'm praying this for _____.

Tonight we pray for the momma who is alone on Valentine's Day. Her spouse may be out of town or deployed overseas, or she may be single. She may just feel alone in the crowd. There are many reasons a momma would be alone on this day. Lord, this year may feel harder than usual. So tonight we pray for her and ask You to comfort her heart as only You can. We ask You to bring her joy and to help her in this moment when she may feel sad. On a day full of love, help her sense deeply just how loved she is by You. We ask for a peaceful night's sleep. We ask in Jesus's name. Amen.

Tonight I'm praying this for _____.

*T*onight we pray for the momma who is fighting for her marriage. She is fighting to stay married because she made a vow "for better, for worse, for richer, for poorer, in sickness and in health." Lord, her spouse may have decided to leave, but she wants to keep working on it. She is not ready to give up. She wants to figure out how to get past the hurt and create a lifelong, happy marriage and home. Lord, tonight we ask that You would give her Your wisdom in this situation. Help her see the full dynamic of everything that is happening around her. Help her find godly advice and professional counsel so she can make a wise decision. Be with her in this storm. We ask in Jesus's name. Amen.

Tonight I'm praying this for _____.

Tonight we pray for the momma who is just trying to do what's best. This momma is always considering the consequences of her decisions. She always takes into account how her choices will affect those she loves. Lord, as this momma weighs all her options, she takes seriously the responsibility she's been given. Encourage her heart tonight to find rest in You. Give her peace in her decisions. Give her hope to face what's ahead. She's a good mom. Remind her of this. We ask in Jesus's name. Amen.

Tonight I'm praying this for _____.

Tonight we pray for the momma who is frustrated. It could be a situation that isn't changing. It could be an attitude of her child or a coworker or her spouse. It could be any number of things in her life that are making her feel as if she is going to boil over. Lord, speak peace to this momma's heart. Remind her that her feelings, even frustrations, can be shared with You. Prompt her heart to share these feelings with You rather than spill them out onto those around her. It's going to be okay. You know it, and she needs to be encouraged in that. Soften her heart now as Your love melts away the frustration. We ask in Jesus's name. Amen.

> Behold, I will do a new thing,
> Now it shall spring forth;
> Shall you not know it?
> I will even make a road in the wilderness
> And rivers in the desert. (Isaiah 43:19, NKJV)

Tonight I'm praying this for _____.

Tonight we pray for the momma who is a safe haven for all who know her. She is a place where others can find rest in everything they've been carrying alone. She is a picture of bearing one another's burdens. Lord, as this momma helps others through their problems and provides wisdom in the hardest situations, refill her cup. Speak life over the weary places in her heart. Bring hope and strength. Help her see herself as You do. Others trust her, and so do You. We ask in Jesus's name. Amen.

Tonight I'm praying this for _____.

*T*onight we pray for the momma who lost herself somewhere along the way. She used to have a goal in mind. She used to have strong convictions. She used to have passion to pursue what burned deep inside her. Her days aren't her own anymore. She goes from one event to the next, thinking of everyone but herself. Lord, even though this momma doesn't consider her own dreams, ambitions, or self-interests anymore, You haven't lost view of her. You haven't lost sight of who she really is. She's Your daughter. Remind her of this powerful truth as You stir up within her a desire to remember the things she loves to do. She is worth her own attention. Remind her of this. Give her rest. We ask in Jesus's name. Amen.

Tonight I'm praying this for _____.

February 20

Tonight we pray for the momma who works outside her home. She is a momma twenty-four seven, and she also gives her time to provide for her family. She might be gone when her children wake up or go to bed, and she might not be there when they get home from school, but her heart never leaves her home. Lord, help her know You see the sacrifices she makes and are proud that she loves so well. While some might question her path, she is proud of the decision she has made. She is strong, and she is a good mom. Bless her tonight. We ask in Jesus's name. Amen.

Tonight I'm praying this for _____.

Tonight we pray for the momma who figured it out. She made a way. It took every part of her, but she got to the bottom of it. That mystifying medical issue, that complicated relationship, that troubling problem at school—she found the answer. Lord, this momma listens to Your wisdom. She knows You can see things she can't. She is confident that You desire to guide her and lead her. She trusts You to point to what she can't understand on her own. Give this momma confidence as she continues to trust Your Holy Spirit speaking inside her. Give her rest tonight. We ask in Jesus's name. Amen.

Tonight I'm praying this for _____.

#MidnightMomDevotional

*T*onight we pray for the momma who has an unexpected pregnancy. Lord, she may have thought she was finished having children, she may have wanted a longer span of time between children, or she may not have wanted children at all. We are reminded that children are a blessing from the Lord. Tonight we pray for this momma as she adjusts to this new situation. Help her find each hidden blessing in this, and give her peace. We ask in Jesus's name. Amen.

> Children are a blessing
> and a gift from the LORD. (Psalm 127:3, CEV)

Tonight I'm praying this for _____.

*T*onight we pray for the momma who is rocking her newborn in the still of the night. The whole world seems to be sleeping, and it feels as if it is just she and her sweet baby and the *click-click* of the rocking chair. Lord, as she prays over this little one tonight, remind her that she is not alone. You know every day of this little one's life, and the prayers this momma will pray tonight will cover her child forever. Give this momma peace. Multiply her sleep tonight, and bless this momma and her baby. We ask in Jesus's name. Amen.

Tonight I'm praying this for _____.

February 24

*T*onight we pray for the momma who suddenly finds herself full of anxiety and worried about life. She may have experienced a trauma, a recent loss, or even an unsettling event, and now she is trying to cope with the anxiety that has followed. Lord, tonight we pray that You would begin to heal her heart and mind and let her peace be restored. Help her step out of the trauma and pain and move forward covered by Your peace and grace. We ask in Jesus's name. Amen.

Tonight I'm praying this for _____.

*T*onight we pray for the grandmomma who is raising her grandchildren. This is not something she planned on doing, but these children bring so much joy to her heart. She loves them deeply. Lord, she is often weary, sometimes discouraged, and maybe feeling overwhelmed. But through all this, You have stood by her side, answered her prayers, and made her strong. Bless this grandmomma tonight. Fill her with peace and hope and renewed strength. We ask in Jesus's name. Amen.

Tonight I'm praying this for _____.

#MidnightMomDevotional

*T*onight we pray for the momma who is awake with her phone in her hand, waiting to hear how something will turn out. She may be waiting to hear back from a doctor or from a loved one who has made it safely home. She may be waiting to find out how the job interview went or what will come next for her family. Lord, You know the outcome of the situation. You know how this all turns out. Give this momma peace and rest as she waits to learn what You already know. It's all going to be okay. We ask in Jesus's name. Amen.

Tonight I'm praying this for _____.

February 27

*T*onight we pray for the momma who can't sleep. She is overwhelmed by the pressures of the day. She is reliving each moment as she thinks back over every word and action. She may feel scared. She may feel guilty. She may even feel sad. Lord, help her mind slow down so she can have deep, restorative sleep tonight. Grant her peace and rest. We ask in Jesus's name. Amen.

Tonight I'm praying this for _____.

*T*onight we pray for the momma who is deployed. She knew this was possible when she enlisted, and she's honored to serve her country in this capacity. Lord, she leaves behind little ones who may be too young to understand why she is gone. Her heart may be heavy tonight, even though she is doing her duty. We pray that You would continue to protect her and comfort all those involved in this situation: this momma, her little ones, the caregivers, and her spouse. Bless them all tonight, and give them peace. We ask in Jesus's name. Amen.

Tonight I'm praying this for _____.

Tonight we pray for the momma who has an empty nest. Her house feels too quiet now that the children have grown up and moved out. Lord, they may be attending college, they may have their first apartment, they may have joined the military, or they may have gotten married. No matter the reason, Lord, this momma has bedrooms that reflect the empty feeling in her heart. Tonight we pray for her and ask that as she goes through this very special kind of grieving, You would lead her and guide her and help her find a new role to fill the void she is experiencing. Give her peace. We ask in Jesus's name. Amen.

Tonight I'm praying this for _____.

March 1

Tonight we pray for the momma who needs to calm her mind. She just can't seem to get it to stop whirring like whistling wind. Lord, tonight help her breathe in Your peace. Help her breathe out all anxiety and stress, and let her mind begin to rest. We thank You, Lord, that every situation she is so worried about tonight is under Your control. This momma can leave it in Your hands. We ask in Jesus's name. Amen.

> He arose and rebuked the wind, and said to the sea, "Peace, be still!" And the wind ceased and there was a great calm. (Mark 4:39, NKJV)

Tonight I'm praying this for _____.

Tonight we pray for the momma who doesn't take no for an answer. When the world says she can't do it, she proves them wrong. When doors close in her face, she makes her own. When everyone around her wonders what she is going to do, she keeps figuring it out. Lord, thank You for this momma's tenacity. Thank You for making her an advocate for herself and her family. She is strong not because she is doing this in her own power but because she knows You are the power inside her. Fortify her for the days ahead, and give her hope to keep pressing on. We ask in Jesus's name. Amen.

Tonight I'm praying this for _____.

March 3

*T*onight we pray for the momma who just needs a minute to breathe. Today came at her hard and fast, and now her head is spinning. The day held many challenges, and tomorrow will bring more. Tonight she is so tired and just wants to close her eyes and sleep. Lord, help this momma give You all the burdens she carried today. Help her place them into Your care until the morning light. When the day breaks tomorrow, let her find new strength and joy as she leaves those cares in Your hands. Help her trust You to sort all this out in Your timing. Bless her with peace tonight. We ask in Jesus's name. Amen.

Tonight I'm praying this for _____.

*T*onight we pray for the momma who spends much of her day taking care of her child with special needs. It is totally different from what she expected when she found out she was going to have a baby. She didn't anticipate changing diapers for more than two or three years. She didn't think about hand-feeding a child past age two. She did dream of conversations she would have with her daughter on her wedding day or college graduation, but those don't seem possible now. Lord, the joy this child brings is incredible! She loves the smiles, the hugs, and the heart of this precious gift. The world may not understand what she faces, Lord, but You do. You knew she was going to be this child's momma. Bless her with strength for this journey. Continue to give her joy every single day. We ask in Jesus's name. Amen.

Tonight I'm praying this for _____.

March 5

Tonight we pray for the momma who wishes there wasn't so much drama. Family, friends, the internet, politics . . . it seems as though everyone has an opinion about everything and no one can ever fully set the differences aside and just get along. She's exhausted from it all. She wishes she could say something to ignite a blaze of peace that puts to rest the fires of frustration in everyone around her. Lord, give this momma wisdom to know how to be a peacemaker. Help her speak the right words to diffuse disagreements and help heal divides. More than anything, give her strength to stand in peace when others war around her. Give her rest tonight. We ask in Jesus's name. Amen.

Tonight I'm praying this for _____.

*T*onight we pray for the momma who spends most of her time with her own thoughts. Her hands make sandwiches and snacks and do the laundry. Her feet go to the store and to the school. But her heart and mind spend time just thinking her own thoughts, and she is so lonely during the day. She longs for community. She longs for deep life relationships that would make such a difference. Lord, You did not call this momma to walk such a lonely path. Tonight we pray for those You have intended to be her community as they begin to connect their hearts with hers. Lord, this is something only You can orchestrate, but we believe You for this blessing. We ask in Jesus's name. Amen.

Tonight I'm praying this for _____.

#MidnightMomDevotional

*T*onight we pray for the momma who needs strength for tomorrow. She is exhausted. She feels as though she used every last ounce of energy to get through today, and she doesn't know where the strength will come from to carry on tomorrow. Lord, tonight we pray for this momma and ask that You would fill her heart with Your strength, just as it says in Scripture. We pray for sweet, restorative rest. We ask in Jesus's name. Amen.

> Those who wait on the LORD
> Shall renew their strength;
> They shall mount up with wings like eagles,
> They shall run and not be weary,
> They shall walk and not faint. (Isaiah 40:31, NKJV)

Tonight I'm praying this for _____.

March 8

*T*onight we pray for the momma who is struggling through daylight saving time and just wants her children to be back on their normal schedule. She is trying to adjust nap times and lunchtime and snack time and bedtime, and it really is all a little too much. Lord, help her with this transition. Give her an extra measure of strength and patience. Give her peace today as she guides her children through this semiannual time-change process. We ask in Jesus's name. Amen.

Tonight I'm praying this for _____.

Tonight we pray for the momma who is discouraged. The stresses of the day seem never ending, and she just feels uncharacteristically overwhelmed. Lord, she is usually a happy, lighthearted person, but this season of trial and stress has taken its toll on her. Tonight we pray for this momma and ask that You would help her find her joy in the journey again. We ask that You would lift the discouragement off her shoulders. Help her find a new song. We ask in Jesus's name. Amen.

> Let us not become weary in doing good, for at the
> proper time we will reap a harvest if we do not give up.
> (Galatians 6:9)

Tonight I'm praying this for _____.

*T*onight we pray for the momma with a mountain ahead of her. She wonders how she is going to climb it because each day it seems to grow higher. Lord, show her that it's not growing; she's just coming closer to it, and she will soon face it with You. This obstacle doesn't intimidate You. You still move mountains, and You still walk with climbers. And just like You walked each of the past steps with her, You are going to walk with her as she scales a challenge that seems too big to overcome on her own. Meet this momma in a powerful way, and give her faith to tell whatever is in front of her to move. We ask in Jesus's name. Amen.

Tonight I'm praying this for _____.

*T*onight we pray for the momma who is in her second trimester of pregnancy. By now, if she's like most mommas, the morning sickness has passed and she has some renewed energy to plan the nursery and prepare for her baby. Lord, if she's still experiencing sickness or lack of energy, restore her body to full health. She's excited as all the details are starting to unfold. Bless this momma tonight as she plans for and dreams of the future. Bless her baby, and please keep them both healthy throughout this process. Give her rest tonight. We ask in Jesus's name. Amen.

Tonight I'm praying this for _____.

*T*onight we pray for the momma who is strong. She doesn't always feel strong, but everyone around her recognizes the strength with which she carries herself and her family. Lord, You have made this momma the woman she is today. You have led her down a path where she has gathered up the ability to press on when everyone else would stop and give up. Offer this momma Your strength tonight. Fill her with Your hope as she moves forward carrying so much. She is brave. She is a champion. You see her resolve to keep going. Help her pass her burdens over to You as she lets go of what's holding her down. Bring her rest now. We ask in Jesus's name. Amen.

Tonight I'm praying this for _____.

March 13

*T*onight we pray for each grandma, nana, grams, gigi, lolly, mimi, memaw, nano, and granny who helps make our lives and our children's lives exceedingly better because of unconditional love and an abundance of wisdom. Lord, whether they live near or far, these precious women add so much to the fabric of our lives. They bring knowledge and just plain common sense to every situation. We are very grateful for the roles they play in our lives and our children's lives. They are each one precious and special. Bless them tonight. Grant them sweet rest. We ask in Jesus's name. Amen.

Tonight I'm praying this for _____.

Tonight we pray for the momma who stands alone. She has little ones to feed and clothe and take care of every day, and it all falls on her shoulders. She is brave. She is a single momma warrior. She doesn't give up. She doesn't sit down. She isn't always strong, but she always acts as if she is. Anything that would harm her children has to go through her first, and she stands right between it and them. Lord, bless this momma who has a fierce heart. Help her know she can rely on You to stand there with her for her children. Bless her with rest tonight. We ask in Jesus's name. Amen.

Tonight I'm praying this for _____.

March 15

Tonight we pray for the momma who has a big week ahead of her. Lord, You know everything she's about to face. You know every assignment she has to take on, every deadline she has to make, every appointment and conversation she will have. You know her exact circumstances. And while it feels as if it's too much for her, we know it's not too much for You. We ask You to walk each step with her. Strengthen her along the way. Give her wisdom to know how to take on each day as it comes. And bring her peace right here on this side of the journey. She won't be facing any of this alone. We ask in Jesus's name. Amen.

Tonight I'm praying this for _____.

Tonight we pray for the momma who has to go to work every day but would like to be a stay-at-home momma. She thinks she is missing out on so much. Her children are growing up, and she doesn't feel as though she is there to watch that happen and to participate in their activities. Lord, bless this momma tonight. We ask that You would fulfill the desire of her heart. Let her find the resources and the path that will allow this to become her reality. We ask in Jesus's name. Amen.

Tonight I'm praying this for _____.

#MidnightMomDevotional

Tonight we pray for the momma who can't seem to catch hold of her racing thoughts. They are flying ahead of her into tomorrow, and her heart is following with all sorts of worry and concern for events that have not happened yet. She can only imagine all the potentially bad outcomes for so many situations. Lord, this is robbing her not only of her peace but also of her much-needed rest tonight to face the actual events tomorrow. Remind her that You already know what tomorrow holds. You are right there with her now and will walk into tomorrow with her as well. Grant this momma sweet rest tonight. We ask in Jesus's name. Amen.

Tonight I'm praying this for _____.

*T*onight we pray for the momma of a teenager who is learning to drive. This is a scary time for a momma. It means more independence for her teen. It means he is out on the road in imperfect weather conditions. Sometimes there are construction zones that bring challenges even to experienced drivers. It is easy for her heart to become overwhelmed. Lord, tonight she needs a special reminder that You are right there with her teen and that You know everything that is happening. We ask for angelic protection as he drives. We ask in Jesus's name. Amen.

Tonight I'm praying this for _____.

March 19

onight we pray for the momma who gave up more than she planned. She knew motherhood would require plenty of sacrifices. She'd sacrifice her sleep. She'd give her time. But some days she looks around at all she has set down so she could carry the love she has for her children, and it feels like so much. Lord, You know the power of sacrifice. You showed us through Jesus that the sacrifice is always worth it. Remind this momma that no part of her love has ever been wasted. You will use every bit of what she's given for the good of her children. Pour encouragement into her heart now. We ask in Jesus's name. Amen.

Even the Son of Man came not to be served but to serve, and to give his life as a ransom for many. (Mark 10:45, ESV)

Tonight I'm praying this for _____.

*T*onight we pray for the momma who is a teacher looking forward to spring break. Lord, she is more than ready for this particular time off from school. She really needs a rest, as the long winter months can be so hard on her in the full classroom. Lord, help her refresh and recharge and hopefully enjoy a little sunshine. Let her rest well on this break so when she returns, she's ready to finish the school year strong. We ask in Jesus's name. Amen.

Tonight I'm praying this for _____.

March 21

Tonight we pray for the momma of a child who has Down syndrome. This momma is part of a community of women from all around the world who love their children fiercely and navigate each special situation for their kids. This momma knows that Down syndrome is just one part of her child's identity, and she works hard to make sure others know all the wonderful aspects of her awesome kid. Lord, we lift up this momma tonight. Wrap Your arms around her and her family. You have a plan for all their days. Help this momma follow Your lead. Give her rest. We ask in Jesus's name. Amen.

Tonight I'm praying this for _____.

March 22

*T*onight we pray for the momma who is so happy that spring-time has finally arrived. She is looking forward to warmer days and to nights that are not as cool. She is ready for her children to go outside and play without having to bundle up. She is ready to put away the boots and mittens and scarves and to let the sunshine bring a brighter outlook to every day. Lord, bless this momma and her hopes and dreams tonight. May she rest well knowing that brighter days are ahead. We ask in Jesus's name. Amen.

Tonight I'm praying this for _____.

March 23

Tonight we pray for the momma who has a heart of generosity and who is always looking for the good in others. Some people think she is too generous, too quick to love, too quick to forgive. Lord, You created this momma to be a representation of Your heart. You created her to show the world what generosity looks like. She does this so well. Lord, tonight we pray that as she rests, You would renew her strength. Help her tomorrow as she continues on the mission You have given her without worrying what others might think. Bless her in her efforts to reflect Your heart. We ask in Jesus's name. Amen.

Tonight I'm praying this for _____.

*T*onight we pray for the momma of a newborn baby. Lord, this challenging season lasts just a few months but feels as if it goes on forever. This momma is worn out, and she sometimes feels guilty for just wanting to sleep. Her body is still adjusting to new hormone levels. Sometimes in the midst of this beautiful season, it all just seems confusing. Lord, if she feels sad or even depressed, help her reach out for professional medical help, which is available because so many mommas feel just like she does after giving birth. Lord, tonight we pray that You would multiply this momma's sleep. Help her rest when she can. Bless her and her little one. We ask in Jesus's name. Amen.

Tonight I'm praying this for _____.

#MidnightMomDevotional

Tonight we pray for the momma who doesn't care what anyone else thinks. She stays in her lane. She runs her race. The opinions of others might come frequently. They might be voiced often. They might come across as very judgmental. But she sticks to what she knows is true. Lord, help this momma remain confident in the direction You're guiding her. When she starts to wonder if she's doing what's right, remind her of what You say and how You are leading. You are so proud of her. We are too. We ask in Jesus's name. Amen.

> The LORD makes firm the steps
>   of the one who delights in him. (Psalm 37:23)

Tonight I'm praying this for _____.

Tonight we pray for the momma who has a dream. She might not have spoken it to anyone else. It might be a dream she has carried her entire life. It might be something new that has been stirring in her heart. Lord, You are the one who has given her the desires of her heart. You don't just give her what she wants. You give her the desire, and then You fulfill it. Help this momma know what steps to take to pursue what You've placed inside her. She might not have much time available, but You can make a way. She might not see how it's going to work out, but You know the next steps. Lead this momma. Fan the flame of hope within her. We ask in Jesus's name. Amen.

Tonight I'm praying this for _____.

March 27

*T*onight we pray for the momma who is scheduled for a C-section for the birth of her child. This is not necessarily the way she planned to have her baby, but according to her doctor, this is the safest way. Bless the doctor and the nurses and the medical staff who will attend the birth. Watch over them all, give them wisdom, and increase their skills in this delivery. Keep the momma and the baby safe. Bless her, and help her not to be afraid or worry. Keep her calm, and give her a special measure of Your grace tonight. We ask in Jesus's name. Amen.

Tonight I'm praying this for _____.

March 28

Tonight we pray for the momma who is battling comparison. She thinks everyone else has it all together or has it easier. It seems as if she's the only one who can't _____, _____, or _____. But, Lord, You see this momma in the middle of her own life. You see the steps she is taking on the individual path You're calling her heart to walk. Remind her now that she isn't behind, she isn't the only one, and she isn't in a place where she should focus on everyone else. She is held in Your love, and You are proud of her. Help her feel proud of herself. Help her see the successes in her own story. Help her focus on running her own race. We ask in Jesus's name. Amen.

Tonight I'm praying this for _____.

March 29

Tonight we pray for the momma who thinks about everything for everyone. Lord, she is doing many things on her own. She is the one who remembers the appointments and the deadlines and what is or isn't in the pantry. She is the one who knows what needs to be accomplished next and when it needs to get done to stay on track. Lord, this momma carries so much. Tonight remind her that You carry her. Help her find rest in You as she lets go of everything she's put on her shoulders until the morning sun rises again and she begins fresh. As she releases it to You, may she feel a deep peace settle over her soul. We ask in Jesus's name. Amen.

Tonight I'm praying this for _____.

Tonight we pray for the momma who is trying to nurse her baby with limited success. She is having so much difficulty that she is wondering if it is worth it to keep trying. She has consulted her pediatrician and a lactation consultant. Lord, she is discouraged. Tonight we pray that You would give her Your wisdom. Help her find the right path for herself and her baby. Calm her heart and help her tonight. We ask in Jesus's name. Amen.

Tonight I'm praying this for _____.

*T*onight we pray for the momma who is undergoing a meta-morphosis, as a caterpillar does to a butterfly. She didn't know she could soar as a momma in all the responsibilities she has. She felt stuck in the mundane tasks of laundry, cooking, and cleaning. But one day she realized she could actually do it all—and with great joy! Lord, we know motherhood is not always like this. But this momma has found her wings, and it has made all the differ-ence in her perspective. Bless this momma who is so joyful tonight. We ask in Jesus's name. Amen.

If the Son makes you free, you shall be free indeed.
(John 8:36, NKJV)

Tonight I'm praying this for _____.

onight we pray for the momma who on this silliest of all holidays, April Fools' Day, is feeling overwhelmed with the parts of motherhood that aren't so silly. Motherhood is not for the faint of heart. It requires courage, perseverance, tenacity, and—above all else—patience. Lord, she possesses all these qualities, but tonight she is just weary and worn out. We ask that You would bless her with sweet rest. Help her heart to settle. Help her little ones to rest well so this momma can sleep. We ask in Jesus's name. Amen.

Tonight I'm praying this for _____.

April 2

Tonight we pray for the momma with a child on the autism spectrum. Every day she faces new challenges and must navigate this complicated path with her son or daughter. This circumstance brings so many extra responsibilities, such as individualized education programs (IEPs), therapies, and doctor's appointments. She sometimes feels lonely and isolated in the midst of all this busyness. Lord, please remind her tonight that You are right by her side. Remind her that You will never leave her nor forsake her and that You love her child. Bless her this night. We ask in Jesus's name. Amen.

Tonight I'm praying this for _____.

Tonight we pray for the momma who needs the sun to rise on her heart. She has walked many dark nights. She has held on to hope through many dreary days, but she needs fresh hope for the days ahead. She needs the sun to shine and melt away all the clouds that cover her heart. Lord, whether it is grief or loss or pain or personal heartache, You know the cause of these overcast days. You know why her heart feels far from the warmth of the light. Let Your light shine on her tonight. Even as the night comes, may she hold on to the promise of a bright start tomorrow. Dawn is coming—not just the dawn of morning light in a few hours but also the dawn of sunny days ahead. Speak hope now. We ask in Jesus's name. Amen.

Tonight I'm praying this for _____.

*T*onight we pray for the momma who is willing to admit when she needs help. She finds comfort in knowing that other adults and professionals are speaking into the life of her child. Lord, she has called on counselors, teachers, friends, and family, and she has created a team around her. This momma knows this is a sign of strength. She is stronger with them, and she is so grateful for them. Bless her, her children, and her community tonight. We ask in Jesus's name. Amen.

Tonight I'm praying this for _____.

April 5

Tonight we pray for the momma who is suffering from past hurts and trauma. The wounds run deep and are not fully healed. Lord, she has tried to move on, but the past just keeps popping up, and she can't seem to let go and forgive. You are the God who forgives. You bring healing in Your wings, and we hide in the shelter of Your promise. Help this momma begin to heal and open her heart to forgiveness for herself and others. We thank You for healing trauma and emotional pain. We thank You for teaching us boundaries that help protect us from further wounding despite our having forgiven others. We ask for wisdom for this momma and rest for her heart. We ask in Jesus's name. Amen.

Tonight I'm praying this for _____.

Tonight we pray for the momma who is single. She is the one who is responsible for all her children's needs. She is responsible for their schooling, their care, their health, all their meals, and the roof over their heads, even when finances are tight. Tonight, Lord, we pray that You would fill this momma's heart with the assurance that You see her struggles and that You are moving in her behalf. We ask for a good night's rest and for her hope to be renewed in the morning. We ask in Jesus's name. Amen.

Tonight I'm praying this for _____.

onight we pray for the momma who is a stay-at-home mom. She spends her days taking care of her children, cooking, cleaning, and sometimes even homeschooling. She is always occupied with the care and nurture of her little ones. She has committed both her days and nights to being a homemaker. Many see her decision as out of touch with current times, but it is the path she has chosen for herself. She is proud of it, and she makes no judgment of the path others have taken. Lord, we bless this momma tonight. We ask that You would give her extra strength and peace in her journey. We ask in Jesus's name. Amen.

Tonight I'm praying this for _____.

*T*onight we pray for the momma whose husband is a first responder. He might have just begun, or he might have been doing this job for decades. No matter how long it has been, she worries about him. The prayers she prays for him don't stop. Lord, this momma needs a good night's sleep. She needs to be able to go to bed with a deep and secure trust that everything's going to be okay, even while she closes her eyes. You are her strength, and You are her husband's shield. Protect her husband as he rushes into all kinds of dangerous situations, and protect her family while he is away. We ask in Jesus's name. Amen.

Tonight I'm praying this for _____.

April 9

Tonight we pray for the momma who is going through a hard trial. This is not a typical, day-to-day difficulty like we all face. This is a hard-fought battle, and it is taking every ounce of her strength and resilience to push through to the other side. Lord, this momma is fighting so hard, but she doesn't struggle alone. She knows that Your Word says in Ephesians 6:12 that her fight is not against flesh and blood but against supernatural powers she cannot even see. Strengthen her spirit as she wars through prayer and praise. Lord, remind her to praise You in the midst of the storm as You push back her enemies. Give her strength for the days ahead. We ask in Jesus's name. Amen.

Tonight I'm praying this for _____.

April 10

*T*onight we pray for the momma who is thinking about the resurrection of Your Son, Jesus, at this time of year. During this season she is focused in her teaching as she raises her children in a Christian home and helps them begin their own relationship with Jesus. This is such a powerful time in the life of the church, and she is using every opportunity to bring her kids closer to You. Bless her efforts and help her as she leads her children to the redemption found at the foot of the cross and then on to the promise of the empty tomb. Bless her tonight. May she have sweet rest and sleep. We ask in Jesus's name. Amen.

Tonight I'm praying this for _____.

Tonight we pray for the momma who struggles with past decisions. It feels as though she can never escape the guilt and regret that fill her heart each day. She feels as if those decisions set her on an irreversible path. She would like to start fresh. Tonight, Lord, we pray that You would remind her that You are the God of forgiveness and second chances. Just as the prodigal son went home and was restored, so will the prodigal daughters be restored to their Father in heaven. Help this momma rest better tonight than she has in years. We ask in Jesus's name. Amen.

Tonight I'm praying this for _____.

onight we pray for the momma who needs the dead and dry areas of her life to be restored. Lord, You are the resurrection and the life. You make all things new. Bless this momma who needs the fresh rain of Your presence to water the barren and thirsty places in her heart. She knows that just as Jesus was raised from the dead on the third day, You are the God who still brings that which is dead back to life. Whether she needs You to move in her home, marriage, relationships, finances, or health, we trust that You are breathing new life into each area. Help her see the signs of life springing forth. We ask in Jesus's name. Amen.

> He is not here; for He is risen, as He said. Come, see the place where the Lord lay. (Matthew 28:6, NKJV)

Tonight I'm praying this for _____.

Tonight we pray for the momma who feels far from shore. The lights on land reveal an impossible distance to cross. She feels as if she's drifting, floating further and further away from solid ground. Lord, tonight we ask that You'd be the anchor of hope in this momma's life. Be the one who reaches out and pulls her to dry land. Be the light that guides her heart through every stormy night. Surround her and shield her. Call to her and remind her that she's not alone. Pull this momma closer to You now. Calm every wind. Speak peace to every strong gale. Help her see where You are right now in this moment. We ask in Jesus's name. Amen.

Tonight I'm praying this for _____.

Tonight we pray for the momma who is in the hospital with a sick child. She may be in the emergency room, in the waiting room, or in a hospital room with her little one. She is waiting for the healing to begin, and she is praying for her child. Lord, You have heard her and are healing her little one even now. You understand that it is hard for a momma when a child is sick at home, but in this sterile and loud and confusing environment, her stresses may be magnified. We know You are with this momma tonight. Help her see the light of Your presence even as the doctors and nurses are helping her child. We ask in Jesus's name. Amen.

Tonight I'm praying this for _____.

April 15

Tonight we pray for the momma whose spouse has lost his job. She may have seen it coming, or this might have blindsided her. Either way, she feels scared and confused. Lord, remind her tonight that You are her family's provision. You will continue to meet all their needs, and You will restore hope and promise for their future. Help them find the exact path You have chosen next for their family. May there be no lack or break in the flow of provision. Give them peace tonight as they trust You. We ask in Jesus's name. Amen.

> My God shall supply all your need according to His riches in glory by Christ Jesus. (Philippians 4:19, NKJV)

Tonight I'm praying this for _____.

Tonight we pray for the momma who feels as though she's not steering her own life. She feels like a product of her schedule and circumstances. Lord, when this momma feels as if she has no power over what happens next, remind her that You are Lord over all. She can trust You to lead. She can trust that even when she feels as though everything is outside her control, nothing is too tough for You. You've got it all. You've got her. Let her rest as You shepherd her heart and her days. We ask in Jesus's name. Amen.

Tonight I'm praying this for _____.

April 17

Tonight we pray for the momma who is up in the middle of the night rocking her baby. She may feel as if she is the only one up in the world. Maybe she is nursing, maybe she is bottle-feeding, or maybe her baby is teething or sick. For whatever reason, she is sitting in her special chair, just rocking with her little one. Lord, during the night hours, mommas can feel so alone, but they never really are. Just as she holds her baby, You hold her. We ask that You would give this sweet momma strength and peace during this midnight season. Help her get rest when she can during the daytime hours. We ask in Jesus's name. Amen.

Tonight I'm praying this for _____.

*T*onight we pray for the momma whose child is involved in sports. It may be T-ball, soccer, basketball, martial arts, gymnastics, or another sport. Her child's activities and schedule create lots of extra work for this momma. She must prepare uniforms or costumes, bring snacks, provide transportation, and sometimes travel to different areas for competitions. Lord, this momma goes above and beyond, cheering on the sidelines. She is a tremendous asset to the team. And she knows that her efforts enrich her child's life. Bless her tonight. Cover her and her child with safety and endurance for the days ahead. We ask in Jesus's name. Amen.

Tonight I'm praying this for _____.

Tonight we pray for the momma who feels as if she is at a red light. She wants so badly to be moving forward. She wants desperately to not be stalled, but she just feels stuck. She can't see a way to press ahead, and she can't find a way to turn around and go back. Lord, meet this momma in this moment. Help her see Your purpose for this pause. We ask that You'd show her that You have her right where she is as a protection. She is with You, and that is the safest place to be. Give her grace as You wait together. We ask in Jesus's name. Amen.

Tonight I'm praying this for _____.

Tonight we pray for the momma who did it all. From the time she opened her eyes this morning until this moment, she handled everything that needed to be done. She made hard decisions. She solved problems. She carried small children. She figured out a way to get her children to do what she asked them to do. She managed the family calendar. She took care of the appointments. She mommed the best she could. And now she just needs a break. Lord, this momma is so much to her family. She is love. She is peace. She is strength. Just as her family leans on her, help this momma lean on You for everything she needs. Give her sweet sleep tonight. We ask in Jesus's name. Amen.

Tonight I'm praying this for _____.

Tonight we pray for the momma everyone counts on. She is always at the school parties or sporting events or serving in the church nursery or Sunday school class. She comes prepared and brings the snacks. Everyone calls on her because she is dependable. It is her joy and pleasure to be there to fill in the gaps. Help her know that she is appreciated, and bless her generous heart tonight. Grant her a good night's sleep because there will be others who will call on her in the morning. We ask in Jesus's name. Amen.

Tonight I'm praying this for _____.

Tonight we pray for the momma who is struggling to connect with her teen or preteen. She tries everything she can to forge a closer bond, but it does not seem to be working. Lord, the child's teen years are hard for a momma. Her child just keeps walking toward independence, and all the while she is sure this teen is not ready. She keeps working on growing their relationship, but her child seems to be working just as hard to pull away and even break down the relationship already in place. Lord, help this momma navigate these difficult teenage years with grace and wisdom, and let her and her child both arrive on the other side with a relationship held together by Your love. Give her peace tonight. We ask in Jesus's name. Amen.

Tonight I'm praying this for _____.

Tonight we pray for the momma who has family members suffering from addiction. Lord, this is the modern plague of our time. It is the scourge that has found its way from the drug houses to main street. It has reached epidemic proportions, and it does not discriminate when it comes to our friends and family members. Lord, tonight we pray for those we know who are suffering because of this terrible epidemic that is sweeping the country. We ask for Your deliverance. We ask that You would save these family members from this dreadful disease. We pray for resources and wisdom and recovery. We ask in Jesus's name. Amen.

Tonight I'm praying this for _____.

April 24

Tonight we pray for the momma who feels as though she is always in a rush. She's always racing from one event, activity, emergency, appointment, practice, pickup, or drop-off to another. She knows other moms who seem to take their time, enjoy their days, and plan their schedules in such a way that they are able to take in the world around them, but she can't figure out how to slow down herself. Lord, this momma needs a chance to catch her breath. She needs to find hidden time in her day. We ask that You would help her find moments to look around and take in the joy of her days and not just race through them. Give her heart rest. We ask in Jesus's name. Amen.

Tonight I'm praying this for _____.

*T*onight we pray for the momma who needs someone to tell her she's normal. She needs to be reminded that her fears and tears and worries and stresses and responses to life aren't strange or unusual. While it might not seem like it, everyone feels the same way she does. Lord, You know she's doing the best she can. You see that she wakes up each day and tries her hardest. Bring hope to her heart as she remembers that it's okay to feel disappointed in the hard days. She doesn't have to love every part of motherhood. She just has to love You and her babies, and she does both really well. Wrap this momma in Your love as You remind her that she's okay. We ask in Jesus's name. Amen.

Tonight I'm praying this for _____.

Tonight we pray for the momma who just wants her heart to be washed clean. She feels stained from bitterness, hurt, regret, and broken promises. She is wearing the pain of all of it, and her heart needs to be made whole. Lord, You made a way for our hearts to be clean. You said if we believed in who You are and in what Your Son did for us on the cross and we asked for forgiveness, His blood would wash away every sin and stain. Tonight this momma is asking You to make her whole and new and to remove all doubt. As she rests her head on her pillow, may she be grateful for the most holy gift of all: the gift of salvation offered freely to us but at such a cost to You. Bless this momma tonight. We ask in Jesus's name. Amen.

> Though your sins are like scarlet,
> They shall be as white as snow;
> Though they are red like crimson,
> They shall be as wool. (Isaiah 1:18, NKJV)

Tonight I'm praying this for _____.

*T*onight we pray for the momma who is ready for the next challenge. Lord, she has completed the assignment You asked her to complete, and she is ready to step into something new. Whatever that is, Lord, we bless her in it. It may be a new job, a new role at church, or even a new season in the lives of her children. Whatever the next challenge is, Lord, You are ready to walk her through it. You walked her through this past season, and You will lead her all the days of her life, safely guiding her into everything that's coming next. Bless this momma tonight. We ask in Jesus's name. Amen.

Tonight I'm praying this for _____.

*T*onight we pray for the momma who is grieving a loss in her community. Lord, someone special to this once-whole community has passed away, and this momma's town, church, circle of friends, or family feels an overwhelming sense of sorrow. Lord, we know the brokenness of this world still breaks Your heart. You weep alongside them, but You are big enough to wrap Your arms around an entire group of people who are suffering together. You are strong enough to bear their pain. Tonight as this community struggles to find a way forward, we ask that You would comfort them, guide them, and be their peace. We ask in Jesus's name. Amen.

Tonight I'm praying this for _____.

April 29

Tonight we pray for the momma who worries during the dark hours. She can manage her anxiety or racing thoughts when the sun is up and the shadows are gone. But as soon as the night comes, she begins to worry. Lord, she doesn't want to spend these hours thinking of everything that could go wrong. She wishes she could just turn it off, but most nights that doesn't happen until the sun rises and the shadows fade away again. Lord, Your Word says in John 1:5 that "the light shines in the darkness, and the darkness has not overcome it." Remind her that day or night, You are still on Your throne and are with her. Give her peace. We ask in Jesus's name. Amen.

Tonight I'm praying this for _____.

April 30

Tonight we pray for the momma who is up doing household tasks while everyone sleeps. She may be doing the final load of laundry, she may be washing floors at a time when little feet won't be running across them, or she may be picking up Legos from the floor to avoid stepping on them later when she has to walk to the baby's room. Lord, bless this momma tonight as she continues to work through the night. Help her know when to let it all go until morning. We ask that You would give her sweet, restorative sleep tonight. We ask in Jesus's name. Amen.

Tonight I'm praying this for _____.

*T*onight we pray for the momma who feels as if she blew it. She had a chance to respond one way, but she lashed out. She had a chance to bring peace, but her stress added to the madness. She feels guilty, and now she is replaying all the moments when she felt as though she fell short. Lord, help her get off the carousel of guilty thoughts. Silence the voice of condemnation that keeps her from living in the freedom You bought on the cross. You forgive her, so help her forgive herself. She's not a failure. She's a good mom. We ask in Jesus's name. Amen.

Tonight I'm praying this for _____.

May 2

*T*onight we pray for the momma who is fighting chronic illness. Whether she is battling an autoimmune disease, diabetes, heart disease, or any other debilitating illness, she still has all the duties of motherhood on her shoulders. She wants to do her best and to be more involved in her children's activities, but she can't as often as she would like because of her health. Lord, she just keeps moving forward, believing for healing and strength each day. Tonight, Lord, we are believing with her. We are standing with her in faith for healing, restoration, and peace. Be her daily strength. We ask in Jesus's name. Amen.

Tonight I'm praying this for _____.

May 3

*T*onight we pray for the momma who needs order in her life and schedule. She wishes she were more organized. She wishes she had a plan she could stick to, but it seems as though everything always reverts to a little bit of chaos and craziness. Help this momma, Lord. Show her ways to streamline what seems so unsettled. Teach her how to order her days so she can get done what she needs to accomplish. And more than anything, give her grace for the days when she just can't find her rhythm. We ask in Jesus's name. Amen.

Tonight I'm praying this for _____.

#MidnightMomDevotional

Tonight we pray for the momma who has lost her own mother. She misses her momma's voice. She misses being able to talk to her and hear her laugh. She misses her wisdom and her reassurance that everything is going to be okay. She thinks of all the things her momma would have loved to have seen or heard about since she's been gone. Lord, this momma wishes she could tell her mom that she is doing well, that she is still going on with her dreams, and that she is still missing her every single day. Be with this momma tonight. Remind her that someday she will have such a wonderful visit with her own momma in heaven. Until that day, help her live her life to the fullest because that's what her momma would want. We ask in Jesus's name. Amen.

Tonight I'm praying this for _____.

May 5

Tonight we pray for the momma who knows that tomorrow could be different. Tomorrow could be the day when everything changes. Lord, while today might be hard and while it might feel overwhelming, she knows she can move forward with confidence in the truth that You are with her. You are leading her. You aren't just standing with her today, but You are also waiting for her in the moments ahead, calling her into the safety of the best route forward. You know the terrain. You know this road. And as she follows You, she'll find that You are a careful shepherd. Remind her that she isn't taking any steps forward alone. We ask in Jesus's name. Amen.

Tonight I'm praying this for _____.

Tonight we pray for the momma who is a nurse. She is on her feet for twelve or more hours a day sometimes. She cares faithfully for her patients and their families. She is so busy, and some days it seems as if she needs two of herself just for the work she's doing while she is away from home. Lord, when she comes home, her children are waiting for her love and care too. And she's faced with laundry, meals, helping with homework, and everything else that a momma does. Strengthen this momma as she does Your work. She brings healing and peace wherever she goes, whether she is at work or home. Strengthen her for the days ahead, and give her peace tonight. We ask in Jesus's name. Amen.

Tonight I'm praying this for _____.

May 7

Tonight we pray for the momma at the end of the school year. When she thinks back to the first days of school when her children were well dressed and their hair was combed and their folders weren't torn or wrinkled, she laughs at how different it all is with just weeks left. Lord, there are end-of-the-year parties and presentations and projects. She may have a preschooler, or she might be helping prepare her nearly adult child for college that will start in just a few months. Wherever her children will go next year, we know You're with them today. You are helping this momma and her growing children finish strong. Give them grace for these last few days or weeks. We ask in Jesus's name. Amen.

Tonight I'm praying this for _____.

Tonight we pray for the momma who is always asked to pray for everyone else. Lord, this momma is no stranger to the power of prayer. When those she loves are in crisis, they call her and ask, "Will you pray?" She always does. When a need presents itself in her community, she's one of the first to be notified because others know she will actually stop and invite You into the situation, Lord. So now we pray for her. We ask that You would meet all her needs. We ask that You'd step in and help her with all the challenges she is facing. She prays for so many, but tonight we lift her up to You. Help her know just how important she is to us. Help her know just how loved and appreciated she is too. We ask in Jesus's name. Amen.

Tonight I'm praying this for _____.

May 9

*T*onight we pray for the momma who has too much to do and not enough help. She sees that what's asked of her cannot physically be accomplished by one person alone. And though she has friends and supporters, she needs even more hands on deck. Lord, send this momma helpers who will walk alongside her, not just in encouragement but also in practical ways. Place people in this momma's life who can help carry her burden. You love her, and You want her to know that she doesn't have to do this alone. She has You, and she has a tribe on their way. Bring her hope and rest. We ask in Jesus's name. Amen.

Tonight I'm praying this for _____.

Tonight we pray for the momma who is a rock for her family. She is the anchor that holds everything together. She is the comforter of broken hearts and the mender of scraped knees. She is the finder of all things lost. She is the champion of everyone she's been given to love. She gives endlessly. She soldiers on tirelessly. She is incredible. Lord, this momma may be weary, she may question her worth, and she might even wonder if anyone notices how much she gives. But this momma is so important to her family. Bless her tonight. Remind her just how proud You are of her. Give her sweet sleep so she can get up and love her family well tomorrow. Show her that she is a gift to all who know her. We ask in Jesus's name. Amen.

> The LORD is my rock and my fortress and my deliverer;
> My God, my strength, in whom I will trust;
> My shield and the horn of my salvation, my stronghold.
>
> (Psalm 18:2, NKJV)

Tonight I'm praying this for _____.

Tonight we pray for the momma who just keeps going. She doesn't quit because she knows what's at stake if she does. She knows she keeps her family healthy by providing nutritious meals and making sure they see a doctor if they are sick. She knows she keeps them financially strong by budgeting and watching carefully over the household expenses. She knows she keeps the house happy and full of joy by her laughter and encouragement and constant keeping of the peace. But, Lord, she knows she is able to do all this because You are her source of strength. Help her remember to ask for assistance when she needs it, and bless this momma tonight as she rests. We ask in Jesus's name. Amen.

Tonight I'm praying this for _____.

#MidnightMomDevotional

May 12

*T*onight we pray for the momma who feels as though she is just spinning around and around, doing the same tasks day after day. Lord, she needs a break from this carousel of motherhood. She needs a few moments to herself to do something new and different. She needs a change of scenery, even if it's just the local coffee shop or park. Lord, tonight we pray that You would give this momma a new perspective. She loves her family fiercely, but she feels dizzy from all the demands. Help her rediscover joy right in the middle of the chaos, and help her find time for herself in the midst of everything else. We ask in Jesus's name. Amen.

Tonight I'm praying this for _____.

*T*onight we pray for the momma who needs her little ones to sleep well tonight. She may have had only a few restless nights, or maybe it's been years since she had a good night's sleep. Lord, she is exhausted, and she knows just how powerful rest can be for a momma's mental and physical health. Help this momma. Help her children sleep through the night in their own beds so she can have a good night's rest. Lord, all kinds of things wake up the little ones, from bad dreams to needing an extra hug or a glass of water to dropping their favorite stuffed animals on the floor. Lord, we ask for good rest for the children so this momma can sleep. We ask in Jesus's name. Amen.

Tonight I'm praying this for _____.

Tonight we pray for the momma who works the night shift. Lord, this momma loves her family so much. Like many other mommas, she does whatever she can to provide for her children. Because of her schedule, she cannot always be home for dinner or bedtime. She cannot always be there to help with homework or rock the baby to sleep. Lord, this momma feels the weight of the road she walks. She knows she is doing what's best. She knows she is loving her children by providing in this way. Remind her tonight that her family appreciates her sacrifice. Her family is stronger because she gives in this way. Remove all guilt, and encourage her this night. Help her know that You are with her as she performs her duties. We ask in Jesus's name. Amen.

Tonight I'm praying this for _____.

*T*onight we pray for the momma who can't shake the yucky feeling that is clouding her heart. She doesn't quite know what's causing it. She's anxious, but nothing has changed to make her feel that way. Yet she feels trapped in a cycle of overthinking and stress. Lord, help this momma tonight. Things are going on around us that we can't see. We have a real Enemy who wants to steal our peace, but You sent Jesus so we could have access to unlimited hope. Help this momma recognize the root cause of her anxiety tonight. Give her restful sleep. We ask in Jesus's name. Amen.

Tonight I'm praying this for _____.

#MidnightMomDevotional

*T*onight we pray for the momma who doesn't want anyone to see her cry. She hides all the hurt and pain and guilt and shame and struggles of each day with a brave smile. Lord, You see every heart. You know each place that is wounded, and the Bible says in Psalm 56:8 that our tears are precious to You. Lord, help this momma know that it is okay to cry sometimes and to let others know she is hurting. Bless her with Your healing grace. We ask tonight that You take away all the pain. May she rest well. We ask in Jesus's name. Amen.

Tonight I'm praying this for _____.

May 17

*T*onight we pray for the momma who is finishing her degree. She set out on this journey to create a better life for herself and her family. She was determined to start, and she is determined to finish strong. Lord, You have brought her through papers and exams and midterms and finals. You have helped her navigate childcare and financial aid. You have told her she is worthy of the opportunity to better herself through education, and she has believed and stepped up to accomplish this great task. Lord, tonight help her rest. Help her prepare for the final leg of this race. When she walks across that graduation stage, You will be right beside her, and all of heaven will be cheering for her as well. Bless her tonight. We ask in Jesus's name. Amen.

Tonight I'm praying this for _____.

*T*onight we pray for the momma who thinks her future is being blocked by her anxiety. She feels as if she can't take a step forward because she is too afraid of what might happen if she does. She thinks and rethinks of all the possible things that could go badly if she makes a wrong decision. Tonight she feels trapped in this cycle of anxiety that seems unrelenting. Lord, You are able to break any cycle of anxiety, unrest, and fear. You are the one who calls us out of our dark thoughts and into the light of Your peace. Tonight let this momma step out of the shadows of worry and fear and into the light of Your goodness and peace. Help her confidently follow You forward. We ask in Jesus's name. Amen.

Tonight I'm praying this for _____.

*T*onight we pray for the woman who is struggling with infertility. Lord, long before she holds a baby in her arms, she has held the dream of a little one in her heart. You see her, God. You know she has tried to get pregnant for a long time. You know she at times feels so discouraged. Lord, tonight remind her that You are the one who builds our houses. Your Word says, "He gives the childless woman a household, making her the joyful mother of children" (Psalm 113:9, CSB). We believe these words for her life. Be with her as she walks out this journey to the moment she becomes a momma. We ask in Jesus's name. Amen.

For this child I prayed, and the LORD has granted me my petition which I asked of Him. (1 Samuel 1:27, NKJV)

Tonight I'm praying this for _____.

onight we pray for the momma who has a momma tribe. Lord, she is so grateful for these women who have gathered around her in this season of motherhood. They are full of laughter and joy and shared stories. They pray with her and tell her their true hearts on any issue. This tribe is tight knit. Sometimes it feels as if they have no room for any more, but then one more shows up, and they welcome her with open arms. Lord, we are grateful for each momma in this tribe. We bless each one tonight. We ask for strength and peace and joy as You build their community. We ask in Jesus's name. Amen.

Tonight I'm praying this for _____.

May 21

Tonight we pray for the momma who goes to battle every day for her family. She doesn't stop, she doesn't hold back, and she doesn't give up. Lord, this momma is strong emotionally, but she is also strong spiritually. She is a momma warrior, and she loves hard, believes hard, and prays hard. This woman is a hero and deserves to be celebrated. We ask that You would bless her tonight. Give her strength for tomorrow as You equip her with Your armor. Thank You for her helmet of salvation and her shield of faith. Thank You that she knows that Your Word, the sword of the Spirit, is her greatest weapon. Protect her and give her peace. We ask in Jesus's name. Amen.

> Take up the shield of faith, with which you can extinguish all the flaming arrows of the evil one. Take the helmet of salvation and the sword of the Spirit, which is the word of God. (Ephesians 6:16–17)

Tonight I'm praying this for _____.

May 22

Tonight we pray for the momma who tried her hardest and did her best. Sometimes she wonders if anyone will remember how much of herself she gave. Sometimes it seems no one fully sees just how much she sacrifices and pours out for those around her. Lord, You see it all. You see every tear, every effort, every choice she made that she believed was the very best at the time. You know she tried her hardest. Clear this momma's heart of any guilt, and give her confidence in who You are within her. Help her hear Your proud cheers. You are such a kind Father, and we love You. We ask in Jesus's name. Amen.

Tonight I'm praying this for _____.

Tonight we pray for the momma whose heart is racing. Her heart is pounding so hard it feels as if it will beat out of her chest. Lord, she is struggling with peace right now. She is in the fight-or-flight mode, and it seems as though she has been running for miles. Right now, Lord, we pray that You would bring peace to her, mentally, physically, spiritually, and emotionally. Help her see Your presence in her story, weaving Your goodness through every place where she has felt alone or in danger. Whatever situation is causing her this much stress, tonight we ask that You'd show her what You're doing within it. We ask for wisdom tonight. We ask in Jesus's name. Amen.

Tonight I'm praying this for _____.

Tonight we pray for the momma whose child has been diagnosed with any chronic condition—in particular, juvenile diabetes. Lord, this is a tricky illness. This momma must always stay on top of what's going on, and she feels exhausted from all the monitoring. Lord, this momma is a warrior for her child. She carefully monitors medications and continually keeps a watchful eye on levels. She feels as if she can't ever fully rest. But she knows the power of prayer, and so do we. Lord, she needs Your wisdom, strength, and resources from heaven to deal with this chronic condition. Lord, You are able to do more than we ask or think, including total healing. Heal this momma's little one, and bless this momma tonight with everything she needs to face what's ahead. She won't be walking this road alone because You walk with her and guide her. We ask in Jesus's name. Amen.

Tonight I'm praying this for _____.

Tonight we pray for the momma who is celebrating Memorial Day with her family, either today or soon. It is a day to honor those who gave the ultimate sacrifice while in military service. Lord, may we always remember that the freedoms we have in this country are ours because brave men and women chose to stand in the gap for our nation. Lord, bless this momma tonight as she remembers perhaps those in her own family who paid the ultimate price for our country. We ask in Jesus's name. Amen.

Tonight I'm praying this for _____.

May 26

*T*onight we pray for the momma who is at the bottom of her cup. She needs there to be more—more strength, more hope, more love, more energy, more peace to pour out. But she feels empty. She feels as though she and everyone else have consumed every last drop. Lord, fill this momma's heart with Your living water. Your love never runs dry, so she never has to run out of anything. Pour Your love into her so that she has enough to pour out on those she loves tomorrow. Supernaturally fill her cup to overflowing. We ask in Jesus's name. Amen.

> You prepare a table before me
>> in the presence of my enemies.
> You anoint my head with oil;
>> my cup overflows. (Psalm 23:5)

Tonight I'm praying this for _____.

onight we pray for the momma who grieves silently. So many think she should just move on. So many don't understand the deep heartache of what she has endured. And though friends came alongside her suffering in the beginning, they don't understand the days, weeks, or years that have followed her loss. Lord, thank You for being a God who pauses to weep over brokenness. You continue to hold this momma close long after the friends and family and well-wishers have gone home. We ask that You'd heal a new layer of her heart right now. Help her feel Your love surround her as You do what only You can do within her. We ask in Jesus's name. Amen.

Tonight I'm praying this for _____.

Tonight we pray for the momma who is worried about her adult children. They may be in their twenties or thirties, or they may be even older. They may have children of their own, but their momma still worries about their happiness and health. She prays for them nightly, and this night is no exception. Lord, please bless this momma tonight with the knowledge that You love her children as much as she does. Remind her that they may have grown up and moved out and begun their own families, but You have remained with them. You are with this momma tonight, and You are with her children. Give them all peace and joy. Help this momma rest well tonight, knowing that her children are cared for continuously by their heavenly Father. We ask in Jesus's name. Amen.

Tonight I'm praying this for _____.

May 29

Tonight we pray for the momma who needs peace over the decision she has made. She prayed about it and asked for Your help and guidance. Lord, she did her research, sought Your wisdom, and reached out for advice from those she trusts. Help this momma leave the decision in Your hands now. Help her trust You because she did her best and she followed You. Give her peace. We ask in Jesus's name. Amen.

> If any of you lacks wisdom, you should ask God, who gives generously to all without finding fault, and it will be given to you. (James 1:5)

Tonight I'm praying this for _____.

Tonight we pray for the momma who needs a break. She needs to get away to refresh and renew herself so she can come back ready to tackle the responsibilities of motherhood. Lord, You see her heart. You know it is on empty right now and she is running on fumes today. Help her speak up and ask for the help and time she needs to get revived in this busy season. Give her wisdom and grace as she addresses this issue and pursues some time away for herself. Remind this momma that there is no shame in investing in her own mental and emotional health. Give her rest tonight, and help her know where to go or whom to ask tomorrow to get the assistance she needs. We ask in Jesus's name. Amen.

Tonight I'm praying this for _____.

May 31

*T*onight we pray for the momma who needs to know that her role as a momma is so very important. She needs to understand that as she raises the next generation, she is taking on a precious and important assignment from You. Lord, we know she is doing kingdom work, even when it seems as if she is taking care of ordinary tasks. Help her see motherhood as You do—as a sacred calling given by You. She might feel as though she is just going through the motions, but she is shaping eternity. Bless her tonight. We ask in Jesus's name. Amen.

Tonight I'm praying this for _____.

onight we pray for the momma who is isolated. She feels so alone. She is away from family and has not found new friends. She may be shy, or she may not have the opportunity to find friends because being a momma is taking up all her time every day. Lord, You set us in the families You have for us. Some families are by birth, some families are by adoption or marriage, and some friends become like our families. Lord, this momma needs a tribe, and we pray with her tonight that You'd surround her with community. Let tomorrow be the start of the end of this season of isolation. Prepare the hearts of those who are going to receive her into their circles of friends. We ask in Jesus's name. Amen.

Tonight I'm praying this for _____.

June 2

*T*onight we pray for the momma who wants a better life and a brighter future for her children. She might be working two jobs or taking night classes this summer. She might have started a new business or be working on developing healthy relationships and community. Whatever steps she has taken, she has decided she wants her children's future to shine brighter and to overflow with possibilities. Lord, bless her on this journey. Fill her with Your wisdom and hope that because You are with her, she will not fail. We ask in Jesus's name. Amen.

Tonight I'm praying this for _____.

June 3

Tonight we pray for the momma who is just exhausted from the day's events. She may have worked, done all the laundry, cooked all the meals, run all the errands, or taken care of little ones throughout the day. She might feel that she accomplished everything or maybe that she worked at everything but accomplished nothing. No matter what she did or did not check off her to-do list, Lord, tonight she is tired to the point of exhaustion. So, we ask that You would help her recharge overnight as she sleeps. Wash over her with Your renewing love so she can face tomorrow with fresh strength. We ask in Jesus's name. Amen.

Tonight I'm praying this for _____.

*T*onight we pray for the momma who is pregnant with her first child. Lord, this momma is receiving tons of advice. So many people want to prepare her. So many friends and family members want to tell her all about the joy she will soon experience on her own. But, Lord, although she is eager, she may also be a little anxious and overwhelmed. She knows this little life is about to change everything, and while she is preparing her heart and her home, she trusts that You will be the steady anchor of this new chapter. Lord, we know You will be with her every step of the way. We ask that You would reassure her heart, especially in the nighttime when worry slips in. Bless her in this amazing and sacred role of motherhood. We ask in Jesus's name. Amen.

Tonight I'm praying this for _____.

June 5

Tonight we pray for the momma who knows prayer is her greatest weapon against fear and anxiety. She knows prayer can change her heart and move the hand of God. She knows it is her greatest tool to defeat the plan of the Enemy. Tonight as this powerful momma cries out to You for healing and brings the things she is afraid of to You in prayer, we join with her and believe for total restoration of her heart and mind. Lord, You are the God who heals. We stand with this momma tonight in Your love. We ask in Jesus's name. Amen.

The prayer of a righteous person is powerful and effective.
(James 5:16)

Tonight I'm praying this for _____.

June 6

Tonight we pray for the momma who helps other mommas. She feels called to walk alongside these other women and help them on their journeys. Lord, tonight she needs Your grace to fulfill her calling. She needs Your strength so she can continue to help hold up everyone else. Sometimes being a helper is easy, and other times it takes everything she has. No matter how this momma feels tonight, whether everything is going smoothly or she feels as if this is all too much, we ask that You'd continue to strengthen her. Bless this momma, and help her awaken fresh in the morning. We ask in Jesus's name. Amen.

Tonight I'm praying this for _____.

June 7

Tonight we pray for the momma who is fighting the battle of how much screen time she should allow her children to have. Lord, so many devices are in her home, from tablets to phones, from gaming systems to televisions, and on and on. This momma just wants her children to truly experience their lives. She wants them to run and play and be outside if possible. She wants them to have childhoods full of opportunities to enjoy the world around them. Lord, these young years are fleeting. Help this momma make the best decisions for her family outside the pressures for more or less of this or that. Give her the wisdom and grace that only You can give. Help her rest tonight. We ask in Jesus's name. Amen.

Tonight I'm praying this for _____.

*T*onight we pray for the momma who can't sleep because she is worried about all the things that happened today and could possibly happen tomorrow. She is revisiting all the places she feels as though she failed. She thinks of the times she raised her voice or was impatient or even just didn't fully engage her children. She worries that tomorrow will be the same. Tonight, Lord, we pray that You would help her find Your peace and be able to fall asleep. Remind her of Your love so that guilt can't steal one more piece of rest or sleep. We ask in Jesus's name. Amen.

Tonight I'm praying this for _____.

#MidnightMomDevotional

June 9

Tonight we pray for the momma who is part of a blended family. Lord, this momma has a unique set of circumstances and challenges. With this growing family come not only more opportunities to show love but also moments of contention and stress as everyone finds a place of belonging. Please remind this momma that it's not up to her alone to make sure this new family works well. It is up to every family member to love one another, help one another, and focus on the places where their lives intersect rather than on the areas where they differ. Bless this momma in this special role tonight. Bless this family as well. We ask in Jesus's name. Amen.

Tonight I'm praying this for _____.

June 10

onight we pray for the momma who is afraid she spends too much time on her phone. Lord, this momma might have small children, and she needs connection with the world outside her home. She might work from home on her phone. She might have relatives or friends who need her encouragement or attention. Or she might just need a break, and her phone is how she spends free time. Lord, there are many different reasons a momma picks up her phone throughout the day. Whatever unique situation this momma is facing, help her look to You for wisdom. Help her truly connect with those right in front of her. Help her disconnect from distractions. Lord, help her find balance, and give her grace as she works it all out. Help her rest tonight. We ask in Jesus's name. Amen.

Tonight I'm praying this for _____.

June 11

*T*onight we pray for the momma who is anxious as the sun is setting. She feels as though she didn't get enough accomplished. She feels as if she failed at so many things today. Now the sun is going down, and she is not ready. *I need more time; I need another chance; I'll do better* is what her heart is saying over and over. Tonight, Lord, please remind her that each morning comes with twenty-four more hours and is another chance at a wonderful fresh start. Let her rest tonight knowing that tomorrow she can wake up refreshed and ready for the new opportunities that You provide. We ask in Jesus's name. Amen.

Tonight I'm praying this for _____.

June 12

Tonight we pray for the momma who has a newborn baby. This is such a wonderful time in her life, but it is also one of the most challenging. This momma is so tired, and she may have other children she is caring for as well. She may have a job to return to, and she may be struggling with the idea of leaving her newborn as she goes back to work. Lord, she needs help. She needs her momma tribe to rally around her with meals and to run errands and provide transportation for the other children. She needs family to help with childcare, and she needs someone who is nonjudgmental to listen to her heart. Lord, bless this momma tonight. Multiply her sleep. We ask in Jesus's name. Amen.

Tonight I'm praying this for _____.

June 13

Tonight we pray for the momma who needs to hear her name. She needs to feel as if she is more than "Momma," "Mom," or "Mommy." Lord, she hears "Mom" called all day, and it can be overwhelming. At times she even feels as if she is losing her identity to the role of momma. But, Lord, You first call her "Daughter." She is Yours. She is made in Your image, and she has Your name and characteristics woven throughout every part of her. She is a woman with creativity and talents and drive and portions of her heart that are not defined by the role of momma. Help her find opportunities to keep discovering who she is under this title that she wears. We ask in Jesus's name. Amen.

Tonight I'm praying this for _____.

Tonight we pray for the momma who is serving You, Lord. She loves You so much. Every day she begins by thanking You for Your goodness, and she does her best to spend time in the Word. She looks forward to serving You by serving others in need. Sometimes she teaches a Sunday school class, sometimes she works with the ladies' group or nursery, and sometimes she helps clean the church. Other times this momma serves You in ways that are outside the church but that help build Your kingdom. Lord, be with her and bring her joy as she completes the assignments You've called her to accomplish. She is a great asset to the body of Christ, and we ask that You'd cover her with Your love tonight. We ask in Jesus's name. Amen.

> His master replied, "Well done, good and faithful servant!
> You have been faithful with a few things; I will put you
> in charge of many things. Come and share your master's
> happiness!" (Matthew 25:21)

Tonight I'm praying this for _____.

#MidnightMomDevotional

Tonight we pray for the momma who is striving for excellence. Lord, she is not a perfectionist, but she's often labeled as one. This momma knows that perfection is impossible to achieve, but she does try to do her very best in every situation. Lord, help this momma know that her best is good enough. Even when she sees the places where she could have performed better, reached a greater outcome, or had a superior result, You know how hard she tried. Help her give herself grace when she knows she has done her best but things didn't turn out the way she hoped. Give her rest tonight as she surrenders every part of today to You. We ask in Jesus's name. Amen.

Tonight I'm praying this for _____ .

June 16

Tonight we pray for the momma who is lonely. She may have the new responsibility of caring for a little one or spend countless hours in her home with napping toddlers or have little ones who make going out stressful or perhaps just be alone during the day while her children are at school. All these make this season of motherhood a lonely time without much adult conversation. Tonight, Lord, we ask that You would be with this momma. Speak powerfully and directly to her heart. Have a conversation with her about the places in her life that need Your attention more than ever. Send people to walk this season with this momma, and remind her that times change quickly and she won't always feel this alone. Bring a deep peace to her heart tonight. We ask in Jesus's name. Amen.

Tonight I'm praying this for _____.

June 17

onight we pray for the momma who is creative. She loves to create new things, whether it is through crafts, decorating, or any number of artsy projects. Lord, being creative is life giving to her. It is such an important outlet. You designed her with a heart and mind like Yours. You love that she's not always organized and she finds time to try new things. Help her make more time for these things that ignite joy within her so she can light up the world around her. Bless this momma so she can flourish. Give her new ideas in her sleep. We ask in Jesus's name. Amen.

Tonight I'm praying this for _____.

Tonight we pray for the momma whose life feels uprooted. She feels as though what was once settled is now disrupted. What once felt secure is now exposed. Lord, this momma needs Your love to anchor her heart. She needs You to remain steady while everything else changes around her. Plant this momma deep in Your protection. Cover her with Your grace. Water her with Your kind mercy. And support her with people she can lean on while everything else takes root. We ask in Jesus's name. Amen.

Tonight I'm praying this for _____.

June 19

Tonight we pray for the momma whose anxiety keeps her from all the important things in life. She has missed weddings, retirements, birthday parties, and all kinds of social engagements because of anxiety. She would love to have a normal social life, but it just feels too overwhelming. Sometimes she looks for any excuse not to go. Lord, we pray for this momma and ask You to help her find the resources she needs to heal. Send friends to walk this often-misunderstood road with her. We pray for Your peace to guard her heart and mind tonight so she will wake with new hope tomorrow. We ask in Jesus's name. Amen.

Tonight I'm praying this for _____.

June 20

Tonight we pray for the momma who is a widow. She has suffered a tremendous loss. And though she is on a journey to healing, she still has days when she doesn't know how she is going to keep moving forward. Lord, You know how much her heart aches. You understand the physical pain of grief. You know she carries the weight of leading the family that she and her husband created together, but You also know she's not carrying it alone. You haven't left her, and You won't leave her. Tonight we ask that You'd surround this momma with those who understand. We ask that You would bring comfort to every hurting place in her heart. Give her rest, and cover her in Your love. We ask in Jesus's name. Amen.

Tonight I'm praying this for _____.

Tonight we pray for the momma who just moved. She is in a brand-new location, and nothing feels familiar. She is trying to adjust and help her children in their adjustment as well. There are new schools, new stores, and new restaurants, and she has not made many (if any) new friends. Lord, this all seems so exciting, but she has left behind dear and precious relationships. She is still grieving those losses and yet somehow celebrating this new beginning. Lord, please bless this momma tonight. Open the right doors in this new season. Help her rest, trusting that You know exactly where she is—no forwarding address needed. We ask in Jesus's name. Amen.

Tonight I'm praying this for _____.

*T*onight we pray for the momma who has been through so much. When others hear her story, they can't imagine how she has been able to endure. When she thinks back on her own journey, she doesn't know how she was able to make it. Lord, You were with her each step of the way. You held her in her pain. You strengthened her in her desperation. You calmed her when she was afraid. You never left her, Lord. Bring a new level of healing to this momma's heart tonight. Heal the deep wounds and trauma from each part of her story. Continue to comfort her as only You can. We ask in Jesus's name. Amen.

Tonight I'm praying this for _____.

June 23

Tonight we pray for the momma who feels alone. She feels invisible to her family, sometimes to her friends, and to those she cares for the most deeply. She longs to be seen and heard. Her heart aches for others to truly understand her thoughts and feelings. She doesn't feel as if she is in a partnership, but rather she feels like a lone parent warrior on the battlefront of raising children and navigating life. Tonight, Lord, we ask that others would see the treasure she is. She's so valuable to Your kingdom. You see her. You know her innermost thoughts. Grant her peace and rest tonight. We ask in Jesus's name. Amen.

Tonight I'm praying this for _____.

Tonight we pray for the momma who has her own business. She is a leader for her employees. She makes the decisions for her company and stands by them. She is a woman of integrity and honor. Lord, You are creative, and You made us in Your image. We ask that You'd bless this momma who creates an environment and work culture that glorifies You. We ask that You would help this momma with all the decisions in the coming weeks. Give her the strength and the resilience to complete her goals and assignments. Bless this leader as she guides her employees. Give her rest tonight. We ask in Jesus's name. Amen.

Tonight I'm praying this for _____.

*T*onight we pray for the momma whose child has complex medical issues requiring specialized medical care. Lord, her precious one may be vent dependent, have a feeding tube, need a wheelchair, or have any number of other special circumstances. Perhaps her child faces genetic components to her issues, as well as physical, emotional, and intellectual complexities. Lord, You understand the entire scope of what this child faces daily. You know every aspect of care this momma takes on each morning and night. This momma doesn't have a break often. She just keeps going, keeps loving, and keeps caring for her child. So tonight we ask that You would cover this momma with Your peace as she walks this journey with her child. Support them both with the best medical team. Bring healing to their home. We ask in Jesus's name. Amen.

Tonight I'm praying this for _____.

June 26

*T*onight we pray for the momma who doesn't know how this is all going to work out. She can't see over the horizon to where the sun comes up in the morning. She tries her best to figure it all out, but she is not sure what the new day will bring. Lord, tonight remind her that You hold every tomorrow in Your hands. Please remind her that You are not just the Lord of today but also the Lord of yesterday and tomorrow and that she is safe trusting in You. Cover her with peace like a blanket so she can sleep soundly tonight. We ask in Jesus's name. Amen.

Tonight I'm praying this for _____.

June 27

Tonight we pray for the single momma who gives it her best every day. She tries so hard and just doesn't quit. She pours out everything she has to offer for her family. Her children are her focus, and her love for them keeps her going forward. Lord, this momma is strong, and she knows You are her source of strength. Remind her now that her best is good enough. Her children are well loved. And help her see that everything is going to be okay because, Lord, You add Your love to hers. And You are all her family needs. We ask in Jesus's name. Amen.

Tonight I'm praying this for _____.

June 28

*T*onight we pray for the momma who needs to hear God's voice clearly. She needs wisdom for a certain situation. She needs to know she is doing okay. She just needs to hear God speaking above all the noise. Lord, You speak so clearly through Your Word and Your Holy Spirit. When this momma's inner dialogue is focused on her failures or her shortcomings, remind her of Your kind voice. Set her eyes on who You are in her and what You have to say about her. You say she's Your beloved daughter. Help her hear Your voice above every accusation of the Enemy. We ask in Jesus's name. Amen.

My sheep hear My voice, and I know them, and they follow Me. (John 10:27, NKJV)

Tonight I'm praying this for _____.

June 29

Tonight we pray for the momma who is frustrated because things don't change. She feels as though she has prayed and prayed for something to shift. She has requested so many times, both silently in prayer and verbally to those around her, for this change to be made, but nothing budges. She does not understand this delay, and she is frustrated. Lord, we ask that You would remind her that You have heard her prayers. You see the fullness of the situation she is facing. Remind her that it is her job to ask You and then to wait upon Your will and good purposes. Thank You, Lord, for Your perfect timing in answering our prayers. Help us rest in this truth. We ask in Jesus's name. Amen.

Tonight I'm praying this for _____.

*T*onight we pray for the momma whose friends are leaving. Lord, she has so much invested in these friendships, including a tremendous amount of her time and her heart. She knows this is such an exciting time for them, and she doesn't want to cast a shadow on their joy, but her own heart is breaking. Lord, You know each of our steps, and they are ordered by You. Please bless this momma and her friends as they part ways. Continue to hold them together in Your love. Soothe their broken hearts. We ask in Jesus's name. Amen.

Tonight I'm praying this for _____.

July 1

*T*onight we pray for the momma who is fresh out of hope. She is discouraged, sad, and maybe even a little worried. She doesn't know how all this is going to work out. Everything feels as if it is falling apart like a house of cards and she can't put it back together again. Lord, You are the God of hope. You are the one who brings new hope every morning. You are faithful to meet us in the new day and fill us with new possibilities. Tonight we ask for a full measure of hope. Grant this momma rest and renewed strength. We ask in Jesus's name. Amen.

Tonight I'm praying this for _____.

Tonight we pray for the momma who never gets a minute to put her baby down. She carried this little life inside her for nine months, and since her little one was born, she rarely has a moment when she is not holding her child. Lord, this momma loves her baby fiercely. Her whole world revolves around this sweet one, but her arms and back could use a break. Strengthen this momma and heal her body. Remind her as she's holding her little baby that You hold her just as closely. You love her just as powerfully, and You never let her go. Give her sweet sleep tonight. We ask in Jesus's name. Amen.

Tonight I'm praying this for _____.

July 3

*T*onight we pray for the momma who has been anxious ever since she can remember. She can think of times in grade school when her anxiety prevented her from doing the things her classmates were doing so easily. She can remember times in high school or college or at her first job when the anxiety overtook her daily life and she found herself making excuses to withdraw from the group. Lord, lifelong anxiety can be difficult to deal with for any momma. So tonight we pray that You would bring her the resources she needs to be healed. Please bring her the tools and coping skills to go forward. She might have always felt anxious, but nothing is too powerful for You. Step in and heal her heart fully. We ask in Jesus's name. Amen.

Tonight I'm praying this for _____.

July 4

Tonight we pray for the momma who celebrated Independence Day with her family and friends. So much excitement surrounds this holiday. She might have enjoyed a local parade, a cookout, or a trip to the beach. She might have hosted guests or traveled or coordinated plans for her family. Lord, she had a lot to think about today. Sparklers and fireworks might have scared her little ones or kept her baby awake. She had to be aware of hot grills, mosquitoes, life jackets and boats, and children running everywhere. The day brought many different challenges. But, Lord, she made it through, and now that everyone is safe in bed, she is ready to go to sleep and rest. Bless this momma tonight, and help her little ones sleep through the noise. May they wake up tomorrow and continue to be grateful for their country's freedom. We ask in Jesus's name. Amen.

Tonight I'm praying this for _____.

July 5

*T*onight we pray for the momma who is this momma's very best friend. Lord, we don't know what we would do without friends in our lives. Our best friends always know what to say, answer us in the middle of the night, show up when we have an emergency, and come through when we need them most. These mommas listen without judgment, love our children as their own, and seem to always make us feel a little less crazy. Lord, tonight we are thankful for this momma friend. We are so grateful for her gift of friendship. Tonight we ask that You would bless her abundantly. Meet every need in her life, and help her know just how much she is appreciated. We ask in Jesus's name. Amen.

Tonight I'm praying this for _____.

*T*onight we pray for the momma who is starting over tomorrow. Lord, today managed to get away from her. But tomorrow is a new day, and she has determined within herself to make it a great one! We are so grateful for new beginnings and fresh starts. Bless her with rest tonight so that in the morning she can rise and be ready for the challenges and joys each day can bring. We ask in Jesus's name. Amen.

Tonight I'm praying this for _____.

July 7

Tonight we pray for the momma who doesn't speak kindly of herself. She says things to herself and about herself that she would never say to her worst enemy. Her opinions of herself aren't very healthy, and she needs someone to remind her how valuable and lovely she really is. Tonight, Lord, we pray that You would help her see herself through Your eyes. Help her remember all the wonderful things You say about her. She is Your daughter, made in Your image, redeemed by the blood of Your Son, and worthy of respect and love. If You wouldn't say it about her, Lord, help her to not say it about herself. Replace her own harsh judgments with compassionate comments. We ask in Jesus's name. Amen.

Tonight I'm praying this for _____.

*T*onight we pray for the momma who cannot make herself feel joyful. She has become so consumed with the major mountains in front of her that finding simple places of happiness on this journey seems impossible. Lord, Your Word says in Galatians 5:22 that joy is one of the fruits of Your Spirit at work in our lives. We cannot manufacture true joy because it comes from You. Lord, remind this momma that no matter her circumstances, she has the ability to laugh and experience joy because it is produced by who You are within her rather than the situations that surround her. We ask that You would restore this momma's joy and let her testimony be that she saw Your goodness in the land of the living. We ask in Jesus's name. Amen.

> I remain confident of this:
>   I will see the goodness of the LORD
>   in the land of the living. (Psalm 27:13)

Tonight I'm praying this for _____.

#MidnightMomDevotional

July 9

*T*onight we pray for the momma who is battling cancer. Whether it is breast cancer, ovarian cancer, uterine cancer, or any other form of this dreadful disease, we lift her up to You. Lord, we ask that You would give her courage in this fight. We ask for those who walk beside her to encourage her, lift her up in prayer, and even help with the daily tasks that are still needed in her role as momma. Your Word says You are the God who heals, and You do not change. So we ask for Your healing power to fill her mind, body, and spirit. Bless her tonight. We pray for peace, rest, and strength for the days, treatments, and therapies ahead. We ask in Jesus's name. Amen.

Tonight I'm praying this for _____.

July 10

*T*onight we pray for the momma whose child keeps her on her toes. She's navigating a very specific situation with this one, and some days it feels like too much. She feels so many different emotions in this season, Lord. She feels dedicated. She feels hopeful. But sometimes she feels discouraged and frustrated. She might even feel guilty at times for wishing she didn't have to figure out these special circumstances. Encourage this momma. Give her strength to care for her child. Give her wisdom to know what to do each day. And tune her heart to Your voice of grace speaking louder than any guilty thoughts she might hear. Help her sleep well tonight so she can face tomorrow with joy. We ask in Jesus's name. Amen.

Tonight I'm praying this for _____.

July 11

Tonight we pray for the momma who needs a friend who understands. Lord, this momma has women in her life who love her. She has mentors and friends and a circle of people who surround her and lift her up, but she needs someone who has been through something similar. She needs someone who has lived through what she is experiencing and can tell her what to expect or how to navigate these waters. Lord, we ask that You'd remind this momma that You understand. You are sending someone who can speak into her specific issues. You are sending someone she can tell everything to and can fully lean on in the days ahead. We pray for the momma who needs this kind of friend, and we pray for the woman You are sending. Bless their friendship now. Give them both peace in their hearts as they rest tonight. We ask in Jesus's name. Amen.

Tonight I'm praying this for _____.

July 12

onight we pray for the momma who refuses to live with regret. She knows what is behind her. She knows everything she has left in the past, but she refuses to let the past call her back into old habits, old feelings, and old guilt. Each day she sets her heart and her face forward, knowing that Your mercies are new each morning and are calling her into a fresh day full of hope. Give this momma confidence for the days ahead as she forgets all that lies behind. We ask in Jesus's name. Amen.

> Forgetting what is behind and straining toward what
> is ahead, I press on toward the goal to win the prize for
> which God has called me heavenward in Christ Jesus.
> (Philippians 3:13–14)

Tonight I'm praying this for _____.

July 13

Tonight we pray for the momma who is a warrior. She doesn't always feel like a warrior, but to all her friends, she is fierce and brave. Lord, this momma has always just done whatever is next on her list. She has taken on whatever is put in front of her. She feels rather ordinary, but she is actually one of the strongest women the people around her know. Tonight we ask that You would surround this momma with Your strengthening love. Hold her up, and help her keep pressing on as she confidently trusts You to lead her. Lord, give this momma rest and endurance for the days ahead. We ask in Jesus's name. Amen.

Tonight I'm praying this for _____.

Tonight we pray for the momma who is brokenhearted. She feels as if her heart has shattered into millions of pieces and she can't breathe because of the weight of this recent news. Lord, she didn't see this coming. Everything was supposed to be different. It seems like a bad dream, and she feels as though she will never recover. Lord, send angels to minister to this momma now. Send Your Holy Spirit to push back the darkness brought on by this heartbreaking event. You are the Lord of hope. You are there each morning with her, and You watch over her each night as she goes to sleep. You are her provider. We ask now that You would comfort her and heal her broken heart. We ask in Jesus's name. Amen.

Tonight I'm praying this for _____.

July 15

Tonight we pray for the momma who is traveling with children. She may be in a car, on a train, or at the airport. Lord, traveling with children always presents a special challenge. Little ones need car seats for airplanes; older children need some kind of distraction such as a tablet, book, or toy; and toddlers need room to move around and just don't like to be confined to a small traveling space for very long. This momma has to consider so many things, and she is trying her best to make sure this process goes smoothly. Tonight, Lord, we ask for traveling mercies. We ask for Your angels to go before them and prepare the way. We ask for no car trouble, detours, or plane delays. We ask for understanding fellow passengers and strangers willing to help should the need arise. Bless this momma and her family tonight. We ask in Jesus's name. Amen.

Tonight I'm praying this for _____.

Tonight we pray for the momma who is trying to find the right educational option for her child. Lord, she is wading through so much information, and many decisions need to be made. She is considering homeschooling, private school, public school, or even a charter school, and she just wants to get this right. She wants more than anything to know that You are guiding her as she finds the best place for her child. Thank You, Lord, for creating each child uniquely and with a special capacity for learning in a particular environment. Help this momma choose what is best for her child. Give her confidence in Your leading. We ask in Jesus's name. Amen.

Tonight I'm praying this for _____.

#MidnightMomDevotional

*T*onight we pray for the momma who received wonderful news today. Her heart is so excited, and she is filled with joy! She waited a long time for this, and now it is finally happening. Lord, we are grateful for good news, whether it comes from near or far. Thank You for allowing us to celebrate with her. You are the God who keeps Your promises, and as we rejoice in this momma's news, we trust that You will be just as good to us. We thank You for every day that is filled with joy. Bless this momma's rest tonight. We ask in Jesus's name. Amen.

Tonight I'm praying this for _____.

Tonight we pray for the momma who shows us that anything is possible. Lord, this momma's successes have taught us that we can dream and hope and start something new ourselves. She might have begun a weight-loss journey, or she might be pursuing her graduate degree. She might have taken on the challenge of starting her own business or beginning a new career. This momma's determination has stirred up hope within us. We ask that You'd bless this momma as she blazes a trail for us to follow. Help her point to You so we remember that You're the source of all our strength. Lord, bless her efforts, and help her know just how proud we are of her. We ask in Jesus's name. Amen.

Tonight I'm praying this for _____.

#MidnightMomDevotional

Tonight we pray for the momma whose heart feels tangled. She feels as if her emotions and thoughts and expectations are all in knots and she can't straighten them out. When she tries to unwrap and sort through one area, she just seems to complicate or confuse something else. She doesn't know where to begin. She doesn't know what to do. Lord, help this momma. Help her find the root cause of her distress. Heal those areas that are causing her to feel constricted. Speak soothing words that are like healing balm to her heart. You know how to sort this all out. Remind her of that hope. We ask in Jesus's name. Amen.

Tonight I'm praying this for _____.

July 20

*T*onight we pray for the momma who has a child with a unique set of challenges. Lord, it might be an attention issue or a medical problem. It might be a behavioral matter or an emotional challenge. She feels overwhelmed by it all, but You care just as much for her as she cares for her child. Whatever it is that this momma does daily to help her child navigate the world, we know You are leading them both. Give them the right teachers and friends. Provide the right helpers for this momma. Bring her peace, and comfort her weary soul. We ask in Jesus's name. Amen.

Tonight I'm praying this for _____.

#MidnightMomDevotional

Tonight we pray for the momma who is suffering from depression. Sometimes she feels as if she can't talk about it because it is often misunderstood. Lord, we know this is a very real illness with symptoms, diagnoses, medications, and therapies. We lift this momma up to You, Lord, and ask that You would help her find the right resources and medical help to bring her mind and spirit to a place of wholeness. Heal every sad, hurting place within her, and help her identify the cause of depression so it can be addressed mentally, physically, spiritually, or emotionally. We are thankful You are the God who heals. We ask in Jesus's name. Amen.

> Weeping may endure for a night,
> But joy comes in the morning. (Psalm 30:5, NKJV)

Tonight I'm praying this for _____.

July 22

Tonight we pray for the momma who needs a pause. Lord, she needs a rest. She needs to think about the weight of her day lifting off her shoulders, and she needs to hear Your voice calming her heart. Help her feel Your tangible presence holding her now. Remind her that it won't always be as it is right now. Lift all anxiety and the stress that came with the burdens she carried today as Your love settles around her. We ask in Jesus's name. Amen.

Tonight I'm praying this for _____.

Tonight we pray for the momma who thought this season in her life would look different. Maybe she thought she'd have more money in the bank or a different job. Maybe she thought she'd be home with her kids or in a more secure relationship. Maybe she thought the places where she needed resolution would be resolved by now. Lord, You know the expectations of this momma's heart. You know the dreams You placed deep within her. You haven't forgotten about her, and while she might have anticipated a different chapter at this point of her story, remind her that You work all things out for her good. She can trust You, and she can trust Your timing. Help her sleep as she rests in this truth tonight. We ask in Jesus's name. Amen.

Tonight I'm praying this for _____.

Tonight we pray for the momma who is in her third trimester of pregnancy. Lord, she can see the finish line in sight. She may be starting to feel very uncomfortable. She may be writing out her birth plan. She may be looking forward with great anticipation to the day when she will meet her little one for the first time, or she may be worried about the labor and delivery part of her pregnancy. Whatever is on her heart tonight, we ask that You would bless her. Please keep her and her baby healthy as they approach her baby's birthday. Help this momma sleep well even with her growing belly. We ask in Jesus's name. Amen.

Tonight I'm praying this for _____.

July 25

Tonight we pray for the momma who swings for the fences. Lord, this momma doesn't care that she has struck out in the past. She doesn't care that things haven't gone her way and that she has faced setbacks in previous seasons. She continues to step up to the plate, points toward the outfield, and says that this time everything is going to work out and this swing is going to take the ball over the fence. Lord, this momma trusts that each new opportunity she faces is another chance for You to show up strong. Meet her right here in this moment. Bless this momma tonight with a good night's sleep so that tomorrow she may wake up refreshed and ready to take on whatever curveballs come her way. We ask in Jesus's name. Amen.

Tonight I'm praying this for _____.

Tonight we pray for the momma who cries alone. It may be in a closet or the laundry room or the car when she has exactly one minute to herself. She is overwhelmed, and she doesn't think anyone sees or cares how much her heart hurts. She feels as if she is failing. Lord, be with this momma tonight. Wrap Your arms of love around her heart, and help her know that You see everything. You know when she is crying and when she is sad. You are with her in every situation, and You weep with her. Comfort her as only You can, and grant her peaceful, restorative sleep so that when she awakens in the morning, she is refreshed for the new day. We ask in Jesus's name. Amen.

Tonight I'm praying this for _____.

July 27

*T*onight we pray for the stepmomma caring for children who arrived in her life through the love she has for her spouse. This momma has such a unique role in the lives of her children. Lord, help her find her place. Help her love as You do—unconditionally. Whether this momma is at odds with the birth momma or they are in sync on this momma journey, working together for the sake of these children, bless these women tonight. Bless this stepmomma as she works it all out with prayer, patience, kindness, and even a good dose of laughter. Help her know that she is a tremendous asset to her family. Help her feel confident in her role. Give her rest tonight. We ask in Jesus's name. Amen.

Tonight I'm praying this for _____.

*T*onight we pray for the momma who loves unconditionally. She is such an easy place for her family to land. She doesn't worry about what people have done wrong; she doesn't take offense, nor does she count offenses. She just keeps showing up for her family and friends. Lord, sometimes a heart that loves so much can bruise easily. We ask that You'd cover this momma's heart with Your protection and heal any hurts. She is a gift to all who know her. Bless this momma and her servant heart. We ask in Jesus's name. Amen.

If you forgive other people when they sin against you, your heavenly Father will also forgive you. (Matthew 6:14)

Tonight I'm praying this for _____.

July 29

Tonight we pray for the momma of a child with food allergies. It might be peanuts, fish, shellfish, wheat, soy, tree nuts, milk, eggs, or any number of allergies that can be life threatening. This momma always must be on guard, keeping a watchful eye and remaining vigilant. Lord, it is a lot to worry about, and it can be overwhelming. Tonight we ask that You would remind this momma that You are walking this allergy journey with her. We pray for resources and wisdom and the right medical team to help her. We pray for understanding peers and teachers so that others will support this momma and her child. Remind her that You never leave her little one. Bring healing and protection. We ask in Jesus's name. Amen.

Tonight I'm praying this for _____.

July 30

Tonight we pray for the momma who is on a journey to health and wholeness. Lord, as she seeks out both medical and spiritual resources to become healthy and takes positive steps toward healing, we ask that You would strengthen her mind and body. She is ready to feel better. She is ready to be able to do what she wasn't well enough to do before. Lord, tonight we ask that You'd encourage her on this journey. Help her find the right path. Connect her to the right group of people who can walk alongside her. Give her rest tonight. We ask in Jesus's name. Amen.

Tonight I'm praying this for _____.

Tonight we pray for the momma who is filled with so much tension that she can't seem to relax. She knows it is not good for her to be this tense, but right now anxiety seems to be in charge. Lord, we know that nothing is too powerful for You. Help this momma see You standing in front of her with open arms. You can carry the whole world in Your hands, and You can carry everything that's causing this momma stress. Settle Your peace over her as Your love causes every tight place in her heart and body to relax. Give her true rest tonight. We ask in Jesus's name. Amen.

Tonight I'm praying this for _____.

Tonight we pray for the momma who is a teacher on summer break. Lord, everybody thinks teachers have easy jobs because they have summers off. But this momma knows that's not true. She is still working on ideas for her lesson plans, scouting out supplies for the less fortunate in her classroom, and attending summer workshops. She is a professional, and she keeps working even when she has no students to teach. Lord, bless this momma tonight as she counts down the days until the chairs in her classroom are filled. She doesn't have only the children in her house; she also has the children in her heart, and she thinks of and prays for them all year. Give her rest, and strengthen her for the days ahead. We ask in Jesus's name. Amen.

Tonight I'm praying this for _____.

Tonight we pray for the momma who is starting something new. It might be a move, a career change, a step from one assignment to another, or a change in roles in her home. God, You know the changes this momma is experiencing. You know every detail surrounding her transition. Lord, give her grace for the days ahead. Give her stamina as she navigates these new waters. Give her hope as she steps into the unknown. Whether she has been planning this new start for years or this change was sudden and unexpected, hold her as the steady, unchanging anchor of her life. Wrap Your arms around her now, when so many other things seem uncertain and unsettled. We ask in Jesus' name. Amen.

Tonight I'm praying this for _____.

Tonight we pray for the momma who has no help. She may be a single momma, a widowed momma, or a momma whose spouse works out of town, is deployed, or works different shifts. There are many reasons a momma may have to do everything by herself. Lord, it is so hard. She feels overwhelmed on so many levels. She needs to know that even if she is physically alone in these responsibilities, You are still beside her, strengthening her. Remind her now that she has complete access to You. You love to talk with her, encourage her, and help her lead her family. Tonight help her feel Your love pushing away all the loneliness. We ask in Jesus's name. Amen.

Tonight I'm praying this for _____.

August 4

Tonight we pray for the momma who has lost a child. The incredible grief and pain in this situation cannot be overstated. She feels as if her world has stopped. The day—the moment—is a memorial forever etched into her heart. Time is tracked as before that moment and after that moment. Tonight, Lord, we pray that You would wrap Your arms of love around her. Your arms are big enough to hold her and her grief. Your arms are strong enough to bear the weight of her pain. Tonight we ask that You would comfort this momma as only You can. We ask in Jesus's name. Amen.

Tonight I'm praying this for _____.

*T*onight we pray for the momma who needs to know she is loved. She needs to know she is loved for who she is and not just what she does. Lord, her role as a momma is all-encompassing. It takes almost every minute of every day, and she can start to feel as though she is not seen or heard. Tonight we pray that You would remind her that she is loved as a person and not just a momma. We ask in Jesus's name. Amen.

Tonight I'm praying this for _____.

*T*onight we pray for the momma who is pushing back fear. She is working to overcome not just her own fear but her children's fears as well. She is tired of fear saying what she can and cannot do. She is tired of fear trying to knock her down and keep her in the depths of darkness. She is climbing out using prayer and Scripture and trusting and believing in You, Lord. We thank You tonight because You are lifting her up and setting her free from worry and fear. Fill her heart with courage and peace. We ask in Jesus's name. Amen.

> God has not given us a spirit of fear, but of power and of love and of a sound mind. (2 Timothy 1:7, NKJV)

Tonight I'm praying this for _____.

Tonight we pray for the momma of multiples. She may have twins or triplets or even quadruplets. She has all the demands and challenges of a momma with one baby, but her workload is multiplied by her number of children. There's only one of her. She has only two arms and one body. So tonight, Lord, we ask that You would send people to be the extra arms and hands she needs to help with the children. She is strong. She is capable. And You knew she was the right momma for these sweet babies. Please grant this momma rest tonight as she works out the schedules for all her children this week. Give her peace. We ask in Jesus's name. Amen.

Tonight I'm praying this for _____.

*T*onight we pray for the momma who feels as though she is swimming upstream against the current. It seems life keeps trying to push her downstream, but she is determined to reach her goal. It doesn't matter to her if everyone else is going a different way. She is charting her own path of motherhood, and if that means she is swimming alone, then so be it. Lord, tonight we pray that You would bless this momma with strength to swim against the currents of the culture and others' expectations. Help her be herself and continue on her own path. Bless her with rest tonight. We ask in Jesus's name. Amen.

Tonight I'm praying this for _____.

Tonight we pray for the momma who feels as if peace is just out of her reach. She pursues rest, but her thoughts and her heart never quite reach the stillness they crave. No matter how hard she contends for a quiet calm in her life, everything seems to spin into chaos. Lord, we ask that You'd walk into the room. Wrap Your love around her like a warm and calming hug, pushing back every fear. When she can't catch up, bring what she needs to her. You're not running away from her. Remind her that You are walking beside her now. We ask in Jesus's name. Amen.

> Peace I leave with you, My peace I give to you; not as the world gives do I give to you. Let not your heart be troubled, neither let it be afraid. (John 14:27, NKJV)

Tonight I'm praying this for _____.

*T*onight we pray for the momma who is sending her children back to school. Lord, this time of year is such an emotional roller coaster of both excitement and nerves. No matter what grade her children are in, those feelings never really stop. They continue all the way to sending her children off to college as young adults. This season can be so hard on a momma's heart. Tonight we ask that You would remind her that You are right there with her children when she is not. You love them and watch over them and protect them every single day. Lord, thank You in advance for caring teachers, friendly classmates, and an easy transition. We ask in Jesus's name. Amen.

Tonight I'm praying this for _____.

August 11

Tonight we pray for the momma who is lonely. Lord, she didn't choose to be lonely, but some seasons of motherhood, such as the newborn stage, just are sometimes. After the showers and reveal parties are over and the activities that surround the birth fade away, the lonely days and even months can set in. Tonight, Lord, we pray for this momma who desperately needs friends and family to rescue her out of this isolation. We ask that You would surround her with a community of people who understand this season and will walk with her through it as comforting guides. We believe You will send these people. We ask in Jesus's name. Amen.

Tonight I'm praying this for _____.

August 12

onight we pray for the momma who is trying to control her future by extensive and detailed planning. She is looking out for every contingency, and she wants to be in control. She knows it is unreasonable to try to control other people's actions, but she still wants to try. It makes her feel safe. It makes her feel secure. And to her anxious heart, it is worth the effort. Lord, You hold her future in Your hands. Tonight we pray that she would begin to trust in You to a greater degree. We pray that she would allow You to be in control as she releases everything she's been trying to manage on her own into Your hands. We speak peace over her heart tonight. We ask in Jesus's name. Amen.

Tonight I'm praying this for _____.

Tonight we pray for the momma whose husband travels for work. He is gone so much of the time. She often feels like a single momma while he is away. She is thankful for the provision he brings and the employment he has, but she is weary of having to do all this alone. Lord, tonight we ask that You would help her find fresh hope in this season. Give her the grace to walk out this journey, as difficult as it is. We ask that You'd strengthen her marriage, protect her husband, unify her family, and give them opportunities to experience great joy in the time they have together. We ask in Jesus's name. Amen.

Tonight I'm praying this for _____.

*T*onight we pray for the momma who needs a break from the daily activities of motherhood. Lord, the cycle of the day sometimes feels relentless. She needs a coffee date with a friend or time away with her spouse. She needs something to help her continue to cope with all the stresses of motherhood in this season. We ask now that You'd help her find a moment just for herself. Help her find time to step away from the routine of the day so she can be ready to love her family well when she returns. Remind her that it's okay to need a break and that it's good for her heart to invest in her own mental and emotional health. We ask in Jesus's name. Amen.

Tonight I'm praying this for _____.

*T*onight we pray for the momma who is afraid. She might be afraid in general, or she might have a specific fear associated with her particular situation. Lord, whatever the case may be, fear is whispering in her ear, *What if?* Tonight, Lord, we pray for this momma, and we say that fear has no voice in her life. Help her hear You saying that she is free from fear, its intimidation, and the stress that comes with it. Renew this momma's mind, and set her free to live her life in the fullest way possible. We ask in Jesus's name. Amen.

Tonight I'm praying this for _____.

Tonight we pray for the momma who teaches the Word. She loves to share God's Word with anyone who will listen. She quotes Scripture during her telephone calls, in Sunday school, on a mission trip, or in a text message. Wherever she is, she is sharing the message of the gospel and reminding others of truth. Tonight, Lord, we are so grateful Your Word is hidden deep in her heart. We are thankful she has it at the ready when it is needed. Continue to strengthen this momma as she stands as a pillar of faith in the lives of so many. Let her have dreams that come from heaven, just as Joseph in the Bible did. We ask in Jesus's name. Amen.

Tonight I'm praying this for _____.

Tonight we pray for the momma who doesn't want to spoil her kids. Lord, this momma wants to teach her children to be thoughtful, kind, compassionate, and considerate of others. She wants them to think of others before themselves and to be grateful. At a time when many people have so much and others have so little, she wants her children to recognize when they have enough to share and to look for opportunities to serve. Lord, bless this momma tonight as she raises her children to be examples of kindness and generosity. Fill their home with Your love. We ask in Jesus's name. Amen.

Tonight I'm praying this for _____.

*T*onight we pray for the momma whose child is going to kindergarten this year. Lord, this is such a big step, and she keeps asking herself, *When did my baby get so big?* Time just seems to fly. It feels as if she just turned around, and now her little one is off to school with a backpack and a lunch box. Lord, please help this momma through this transition. Remind her that You go with her kindergartener, even though she can't. Help her little one as they take this next big step. Give them peace and joy in this season. We ask in Jesus's name. Amen.

Tonight I'm praying this for _____.

*T*onight we pray for the momma who has a hard time after sundown. It seems as if the world is a bigger and scarier place once the sun sets and the shadows appear. It feels as though the things that worry her the most grow bigger in the shadows of the evening and midnight hours. Lord, be with this momma tonight. Remind her that You are the light of the world. With You there is no shadow of turning. You create peace with the light of Your presence. We pray for rest and for all worry and fear to leave tonight. We ask in Jesus's name. Amen.

Tonight I'm praying this for _____.

August 20

*T*onight we pray for the momma who needs an answer. She has asked and asked in prayer but does not feel as if the answer has come. Lord, You know all our steps. You give wisdom generously to all those who ask, according to James 1:5. As this momma awaits her answer and direction from You, we ask that You would bring her the peace and assurance she needs to remember that it is all in Your hands. You are always right on time. Help this momma have patience as she waits for You. We ask in Jesus's name. Amen.

Tonight I'm praying this for _____.

*T*onight we pray for the momma who is sending her first child off to college. She may still have children at home, but this first one is so hard to let go of for so long. She knows that everything will change when she leaves her baby on campus. She knows that curfews and meals and study times will all become her grown child's responsibility, and she is a little worried about how it will all be accomplished. Lord, remind her that You love her child just as much as she does and that You will always be with both of them. You hold them together with Your love no matter how far apart they are. Bless them with rest tonight. We ask in Jesus's name. Amen.

Tonight I'm praying this for _____.

#MidnightMomDevotional

August 22

*T*onight we pray for the momma with a rainbow pregnancy. Lord, she is so excited about having this baby, but she is very nervous because of a previous miscarriage or stillbirth. You see this momma's heart and understand the trauma she went through the last time she was pregnant. Lord, You bind our wounds and heal our hearts. Help this momma rest in Your love for her tonight. We know she will always have a place in her heart for the one who went to Your arms early, but strengthen her hope as she looks to the future now. Bless this momma tonight. We ask in Jesus's name. Amen.

Tonight I'm praying this for _____.

Tonight we pray for the momma who is anxious about world events. It seems as if this world is spinning out of control. The nightly news and social media present every issue imaginable to worry about. She can't ignore these issues because they are right there every day. She feels powerless to bring about any kind of real change in these events. Lord, the only way a momma can really change world history is by influencing the lives of her children. Show her that by raising these precious little ones, she is reaching into the future and saying it will be better because these little lives will have a positive impact on it. Bless her tonight in the greatest calling: that of motherhood. We ask in Jesus's name. Amen.

Tonight I'm praying this for _____.

August 24

*T*onight we pray for the momma who is about to have her baby. Her due date is near, the doctors have decided to induce, or she has a scheduled C-section. Lord, it is an amazing process to give birth, but it can also be a time of anxiousness and worry. Please calm her momma heart, and give her the assurance she needs to get through the birth. Protect her and her baby. Prepare the hearts of those who will care for her medically and emotionally during this beautiful process of birthing new life. Give her peace. We ask in Jesus's name. Amen.

Tonight I'm praying this for _____.

August 25

*T*onight we pray for the momma who feels as though her faith is wavering. Lord, she is believing You will help her with her children and many other things, but tonight her faith feels unsteady. Please remind her that her faith is built on You, the rock of our salvation. Please remind her that even though she is worried, You are her steady hand. You hold her up and give her strength. Help her in this hour of need as she holds firmly to the promises You have made to her in Your Word. You said to Simon Peter that his faith would not fail. We believe You're saying the same thing to this momma. Strengthen her now. We ask in Jesus's name. Amen.

I have prayed for you, Simon, that your faith may not fail. (Luke 22:32)

Tonight I'm praying this for _____.

August 26

*T*onight we pray for the momma who is adjusting to life with her newborn. She is gaining confidence daily, but at times she feels as if she still has no idea what she's doing. So many choices need to be made. So many options are available. And so many voices are telling her how she should be doing it all. Lord, give this momma not only wisdom to know what to do but also confidence in her mothering. She has You as a guide and trusted friend. She can count on You to help her with each step she takes. Give her peace and rest. Bless her tonight. We ask in Jesus's name. Amen.

Tonight I'm praying this for _____.

August 27

Tonight we pray for the momma who has a secret. Lord, she might have news she cannot share with anyone else. She feels the weight of this burden that only she knows about, and it overwhelms her. Or, Lord, she may have been carrying this secret for so long that sometimes she forgets it. This secret brings her pain and causes her to doubt herself. She wishes she could bring it into the light so she could be free from suffering in silence. Lord, You know every heart and every thought. Nothing is hidden from You, and yet Your love does not change. Help this momma give You the weight of this situation as she trusts that You will lead her and strengthen her and bring her peace. Surround her with Your love. We ask in Jesus's name. Amen.

Tonight I'm praying this for _____.

#MidnightMomDevotional

Tonight we pray for the momma who is worried about sending her children to school because of all the violence that has happened in classrooms across the nation. She is worried because she is not there to take care of her children, and it makes her afraid to think of the unthinkable happening in their building. Lord, she trusts You with her children. So please help this momma rest tonight. Remind her that in all situations, You are right there with the ones she loves most. You never leave or forsake them. Fill her heart with peace. We ask in Jesus's name. Amen.

Tonight I'm praying this for _____.

August 29

*T*onight we pray for the momma who just can't see how every-thing is going to work out in the end. She keeps asking her-self, *What if it doesn't?* She looks around at her situation and sees the difficulties and the hardship, and she wonders what will hap-pen next. Lord, You know this momma's destiny. You know every single one of her days. It says in Psalm 139:16, "All the days or-dained for me were written in your book before one of them came to be." Lord, You know the end from the beginning and every day in between. Help her trust tonight that You have a good plan for her life. We ask in Jesus's name. Amen.

Tonight I'm praying this for _____.

August 30

*T*onight we pray for the momma who coordinates the nursery or preschool at church. This momma is special to so many families. She is a constant source of love for the little ones who know her and for their mommas who count on her. Thank You, Lord, for showing this momma how to reveal Your heart to the little ones You love so much. Help her know just how loved and appreciated she is by all who know her. Fill her home with Your love. Give her sweet rest tonight. We ask in Jesus's name. Amen.

Tonight I'm praying this for _____.

*T*onight we pray for the momma who is waiting for news. It may be good news or not-so-good news, but the waiting is keeping her awake tonight. Lord, You know everything. The Bible says in Psalm 37:23 that the steps of the righteous are ordered by the Lord. Tonight, Lord, we believe that You have ordered her steps. Whatever the news is, You knew it before the beginning of time and prepared her to receive it. We ask that You'd give this momma the ability to discern what to do next in this circumstance. Strengthen her spirit, and encourage her as she waits for You. We ask in Jesus's name. Amen.

Tonight I'm praying this for _____.

Tonight we pray for the momma who can hear Jesus calling to her but doesn't know how to respond. She senses the Lord wants her to move forward, but she can't hear clearly enough to know where or how. Lord, just as You called Lazarus out of the grave and he came back to life, You call this momma out of her pain, her sadness, her anxiety. You call her out of hopelessness. You call her into life. Help her trust that all she has to do is take a step toward You and she will be taking a step toward her future. Bless this momma. Give her courage to leave the grave behind. We ask in Jesus's name. Amen.

Tonight I'm praying this for _____.

*T*onight we pray for the momma who has an anxious child. Lord, the things that come easily for some children may seem impossible for this one. He tries his hardest to overcome his fears and do all the things that other kids do and that his little heart wants to do. Some days, Lord, it is just too much. Tonight we pray for this momma as she navigates this complex issue of childhood anxiety. Every path to health is a little different. Help this momma find the right path for her child. Send her the resources necessary to succeed. Fill their home with peace. We ask in Jesus's name. Amen.

Tonight I'm praying this for _____.

September 3

*T*onight we pray for the momma who doesn't get invited to the girls' group. She doesn't have a big circle of friends who take her out to lunch or invite her over to watch that one television show everyone is watching. She feels excluded, and she wonders if something is wrong with her. She questions why she doesn't get that text or invite. Lord, she is a good friend. She is a reliable friend. She is someone others can count on. Help her see just how much she contributes to those around her. Help her realize she is wanted and welcomed by those who take the time to get to know her. Help her become the one who invites other women to the table. We ask in Jesus's name. Amen.

Tonight I'm praying this for _____.

*T*onight we pray for the single momma who is managing the back-to-school routine by herself. She has purchased all the school supplies, all the new shoes, all the new clothes and backpacks. It has been a real strain on the budget, but she wants her children to have a good start to this new school year. Lord, she does all the things her children require help with, from packing lunches and overseeing homework to getting them to sports practices and dance recitals. Tonight, Lord, we ask for a special blessing for this momma. Please give her Your strength to continue to do her very best. She is a single momma warrior. Bless her rest tonight. We ask in Jesus's name. Amen.

Tonight I'm praying this for _____.

#MidnightMomDevotional

September 5

*T*onight we pray for the momma who is just tired of the day-to-day routine. She wants something exciting to happen to shake up the ordinary. She feels ready for a change. Tonight, Lord, we ask that You would help this momma see her everyday life with new eyes. We pray that You would bring the wonder of motherhood back to this momma. Help her find her spark of joy again. Help her not to drift through life, waiting for the next exciting thing, but to see the beauty in everything that surrounds her. We ask that You would bless her with sweet sleep tonight so she may wake up in the morning refreshed for the daily routine that is motherhood. We ask in Jesus's name. Amen.

Tonight I'm praying this for _____.

*T*onight we pray for the momma who is a teacher just beginning a new school year. She knows that the excitement of new backpacks and lunch boxes and pencil cases will soon wear off, but she is enjoying meeting her new students and developing her lesson plans with them in mind. Lord, bless her in this new season. This year we ask for Your Spirit to assist her as she helps her students learn. We thank You that she is a true professional who focuses on the success of all the children in her classroom. We are grateful that she chose teaching as her profession. Help her rest well tonight and be ready for a new day in the morning. We ask in Jesus's name. Amen.

Tonight I'm praying this for _____.

September 7

*T*onight we pray for the momma who wishes she could spend more time with her adult children. Lord, when they were little, it seemed as though she rarely had a break. She longed for just a moment to herself when she could rest her mind from all the questions and needs. Now she'd do anything to find just a little more time to sit and listen to what is happening in the lives of her grown children and to help with anything she can. Help this momma's heart find joy in the new season of life. Help her and her children find moments to connect in new ways. This momma has sown many important seeds of relationship into her children. We pray these seeds would bloom into a garden that they'd enjoy together now. Give this momma rest. We ask in Jesus's name. Amen.

Tonight I'm praying this for _____.

Tonight we pray for the momma bear. Lord, she is protective and fierce. She always defends her children no matter the cost and stands up for what's right for her family. This momma puts up with no nonsense and knows that her instinct to protect is such a valuable asset to her family and friends. Everyone who knows her recognizes that she is the go-to mom in any situation that requires someone to be brave and honest. We ask that You'd bless her tonight and help her see the high importance of her role in her family and community. We ask in Jesus's name. Amen.

Tonight I'm praying this for _____.

September 9

Tonight we pray for the momma who wants her home to be a place of refuge. Lord, she wants her family to feel accepted, loved, and peaceful when they walk through the front door. She works hard for this every day. She tries to create a warm and welcoming environment for both family and friends. Sometimes it's candles, soft music, the smell of fresh bread from the oven, or an extra throw or pillow on the sofa to add to the peaceful tone. Tonight, Lord, as You fill her home once again with Your love, help her family sense Your presence. Give them sweet dreams and peaceful thoughts as they rest knowing that You are with them. We ask in Jesus's name. Amen.

> The name of the LORD is a strong tower;
> The righteous run to it and are safe. (Proverbs 18:10, NKJV)

Tonight I'm praying this for _____.

September 10

Tonight we pray for the momma whose child is in college. Lord, she wants her child to succeed and to have opportunities for a productive and fulfilling career that would not be available without a college degree. She knows college life is a big adjustment with fewer rules, greater opportunities to make mistakes, and less supervision. We pray for understanding professors, roommates who are a good fit, and adequate time for studies. As her child makes lifelong friendships, we ask for Your guidance and blessings. Lord, tonight be with this momma as she prays for her child. Hear her prayers, and grant her the wisdom she needs to help her college student through this transitional season to adulthood. We ask in Jesus's name. Amen.

Tonight I'm praying this for _____.

*T*onight we pray for the momma who always takes what life gives her and makes something beautiful out of it. She knows how to stretch and bend and create and take whatever comes her way and turn it into something to be proud of. Lord, this momma might not have always had it easy, but she makes it look easy to everyone around her. She might have had to work for what she has, but she appreciates everything around her because she knows she played a part in making it all that it is. Thank You for this momma's passion. Thank You for her wit. Thank You for her determination. Bless her tonight. We ask in Jesus's name. Amen.

Tonight I'm praying this for _____.

September 12

Tonight we pray for the momma who is tired. Lord, she would like to just close her eyes and sleep until she wakes up in the morning, completely rested. She knows that won't be possible tonight. Either her baby is sick, her older child has been having nightmares, her teenager is still out with her friends, or her young adult is still at work. Lord, there are so many reasons mommas don't sleep at night, and we know You see them all. We ask that You would multiply whatever sleep this momma is able to get so it is sufficient for tomorrow. Let her trust You with her specific situation tonight. We ask in Jesus's name. Amen.

> I will both lie down in peace, and sleep;
> For You alone, O LORD, make me dwell in safety.
> (Psalm 4:8, NKJV)

Tonight I'm praying this for _____.

September 13

onight we pray for the momma who is struggling with secondary infertility. She already has been pregnant and now is trying to get pregnant again, but this time seems more difficult. The time that has passed since the birth of her first child feels too long, and she doesn't quite know what to do about it. Lord, she is trying to figure out if it is Your will for her to have more children. She is wondering if not being able to get pregnant again is a sign. Tonight, Lord, we pray that You would speak to her momma heart. Speak the words she needs to hear from You in order to know what she is supposed to do next. Grant her wisdom in this season. Bring her joy and peace. We ask in Jesus's name. Amen.

Tonight I'm praying this for _____.

*T*onight we pray for the momma who feels the pressure of anxiety every day. She may have an underlying physical condition that makes her anxious, she may have a genetic disorder, or she may have PTSD from a traumatic event. Lord, for whatever reason, every day she carries the weight of anxiety on her shoulders and in her heart. She wants to be the fun-loving momma, the momma who smiles and laughs and enjoys everyday life. But the weight of this anxiety takes the joy out of most days. Tonight, Lord, we ask that You would remind this momma that she is not alone. You are with her every step of every day. Please bring Your healing grace. Help her find the resources she needs to be healed and the strength to keep looking until she finds them. We ask in Jesus's name. Amen.

> The peace of God, which transcends all understanding,
> will guard your hearts and your minds in Christ Jesus.
> (Philippians 4:7)

Tonight I'm praying this for _____.

September 15

*T*onight we pray for the momma who is starting a new job. Lord, she is excited about the new possibilities this opportunity offers. She knows she has the skills and the credentials to do a great job, but she is a little nervous. Lord, bless the work of her hands and heart. As she sets her face to this new horizon, give her a tremendous sense of accomplishment as You expand her boundaries toward new territory. You have been preparing her for this moment. Lord, we thank You for new beginnings. Help her rest well tonight for tomorrow's challenges. We ask in Jesus's name. Amen.

Tonight I'm praying this for _____.

Tonight we pray for the momma whose little one is going to prekindergarten. Lord, this is the first time her child will be in a daily group setting, and this is the first time someone else will have the responsibility of caring for her child for an extended period of time. She is overwhelmed with the what-ifs. She is worried that something won't be perfect and she won't be there to fix it. She is worried about her child getting hurt on the playground. There is so much she is unsure of. Lord, touch this momma's heart, and bring her peace. Remind her that You will be right there with her little one. Give her rest tonight. We ask in Jesus's name. Amen.

Tonight I'm praying this for _____.

September 17

Tonight we pray for the momma who is helping her child fall asleep on his own. Lord, she is trying to develop a new routine. Her little one may be moving to a new bed or a different room, or she may be helping him fall asleep without needing to be rocked. She may be trying to move out of the doorway of her child's room, where he must see her until he nods off. Lord, please help this momma as she walks this new path. She is trying to do what's right for her child and her whole family, but situations like this can be so stressful. Meet them right where they are tonight, God. Bring peace to this little one and this momma. Help them all sleep well. We ask in Jesus's name. Amen.

Tonight I'm praying this for _____.

*T*onight we pray for the momma of the child in middle school. Lord, this is such a unique time when children begin to decide what their future will look like. Picking out electives such as band or drama not only defines a child's educational path but also sometimes determines her circle of friends, and it seems so early in life for her to be making these big decisions. Lord, this momma wants to help and guide her child, but she also wants her child to find her own voice and begin to discover her future. Lord, please be with this momma as she walks this journey with her child. Give her Your wisdom and grace for every decision. Please guard this child's destiny as we cover it in prayer. We ask in Jesus's name. Amen.

Tonight I'm praying this for _____.

September 19

Tonight we pray for the momma who needs to get her laugh back. Lord, she used to be carefree and laugh easily. She found joy in so much. She looked forward to being a momma and knew it would be full of opportunities to love and laugh. But, Lord, sometimes these days have been more trying than she expected. She has experienced more love than she ever imagined, but she has also felt pressure to get it all right. Lord, this momma needs her joy to return. She needs You to fill her heart with hope. She needs rest, and she needs You to lift the weight of tomorrow so she can laugh today. We ask in Jesus's name. Amen.

Tonight I'm praying this for _____.

September 20

*T*onight we pray for the momma who has not found her tribe. Lord, she is doing this season of motherhood alone. She needs a group of women she can trust to share this journey every day, but for some reason she has not found it yet. Tonight we ask for fresh ideas on how to make new friends. Help her trust in You as You open new doors of friendship for her. Lord, we pray for wisdom. We ask that You would show her what authentic community looks like. Help her reach out and not be afraid. We ask in Jesus's name. Amen.

Tonight I'm praying this for _____.

September 21

*T*onight we pray for the momma who doesn't feel as if life prepared her to take on motherhood. She didn't have the support or the training or the family structure to learn from. She feels as if she's just figuring it out herself, and most days she wonders if she's doing a good enough job. Lord, through You, we have everything we need. You know this momma's story and her history, and You placed her children in her arms. Help her trust in You as she is figuring this out. You are leading her; in this she can be confident. Give her rest tonight. We ask in Jesus's name. Amen.

Tonight I'm praying this for _____.

September 22

*T*onight we pray for the momma who is a stepmomma. This is such a unique role that has to be walked like a tightrope. She wants to respect the children's birth momma, with whom she shares parenting duties even though she is not in the home. This can be both exhausting and challenging. It can be fulfilling to assist in raising another's children, but sometimes it can be overwhelming. Tonight we pray for wisdom for this stepmomma. Help her overcome whatever obstacles are in her way so she can become the best stepparent possible. Help her rest tonight, and grant her Your wisdom for tomorrow. We ask in Jesus's name. Amen.

Tonight I'm praying this for _____.

*T*onight we pray for the momma of the child who is being bullied. Lord, she has asked for help from the school and in some cases even the authorities. We pray they are all working together to stop the bullying. But, Lord, this momma is heartbroken for her child. She is so upset that he is being harassed at school or by neighborhood bullies or even online. She wants her little one to be accepted and loved for who he is. She doesn't want him to be shut out and bullied. Lord, this is a difficult and heartbreaking situation, so we pray for guidance and peace for this momma and her child. We ask that You would bring Your healing grace to this situation. We ask in Jesus's name. Amen.

Tonight I'm praying this for _____.

September 24

*T*onight we pray for the momma who remains hopeful. It might seem bleak to others. It might seem completely hopeless to some. But this momma, despite what her circumstances say, knows that God is with her. Lord, remind this momma that if her hope is found in You, it is secure. Remind her that You aren't going to leave her. Reassure her that everything could change for the better, and show her the ways it could improve. She is a beacon of hope for all those around her. Strengthen her as she trusts in You. We ask in Jesus's name. Amen.

Tonight I'm praying this for _____.

September 25

onight we pray for the momma who has always been prepared to go any distance for her children. She'd climb a mountain barefoot if it meant health or hope or a future for her children. She'd make hard choices and painful sacrifices to care for the ones she's been given to love. Lord, this momma is a picture of strength and dedication. But she also needs to think about her own mental, emotional, and physical health. Sometimes the sacrifices wear on her, and she needs You to restore the worn places in her heart, mind, and body. Send Your Spirit, Lord, to minister to her now. Bring peace. Bring hope. Bring everything she needs, including sleep tonight. We ask in Jesus's name. Amen.

Tonight I'm praying this for _____.

*T*onight we pray for the momma who woke up today knowing that not much would have changed since she laid her head down last night. Every day feels basically the same. She spent today doing a lot of the same things she does every day: cooking, cleaning, and running errands. Lord, this momma needs a surprise. She needs something new to happen to spark excitement in her days. She's content, and she's faithful to keep everything running for her family. But, Lord, would You bless this momma with something fun and unexpected? Send her a visit from a friend or a text or something to let her know that she is seen and valued and that each day holds its own unplanned gifts. Please help her rest well tonight. We ask in Jesus's name. Amen.

Tonight I'm praying this for _____.

September 27

*T*onight we pray for the momma who is suffering from panic attacks. These can be so scary, and she doesn't know when they will happen. She can be in the grocery store or at work or even at school, and suddenly she feels overwhelmed and can't breathe. Lord, help this momma find the resources she needs to be completely whole. Guide her to the right doctors, counselors, and friends who can help her heal. Help her discover the root cause of these attacks. We pray for Your peace to overwhelm her heart to a greater degree than the panic does. We ask for Your help in this situation. We ask in Jesus's name. Amen.

Tonight I'm praying this for _____.

*T*onight we pray for the momma who is worried about finances. Her spouse may have lost his job, she may be a single momma who lost her job, or perhaps the paycheck this week just wasn't big enough. She may have an unexpected expense, such as a car repair or a visit to the doctor. Lord, whatever issue her family is facing, please remind her that You are right there with her. Your Word says You clothe the lilies of the field and know when a sparrow falls to the earth. You are with us in every situation, and You understand all our financial needs. Help this momma trust You with her family's finances. We ask in Jesus's name. Amen.

Tonight I'm praying this for _____.

Tonight we pray for the momma who just can't imagine how this sea in front of her will split so she can cross it safely. She feels as if time is running out and she needs an answer ASAP. She is starting to panic. She feels desperate. Lord, You stand right next to this momma. You are the same God who told Moses to hold up his staff as You parted the Red Sea in front of him. Remind this momma that You have a way forward even when she can't see it. You didn't bring her to this place to forget about her. You have led her safely this far, even when the road was scary. And You will lead her safely on. Make a way for her, Lord, and give her rest tonight. We ask in Jesus's name. Amen.

Tonight I'm praying this for _____.

Tonight we pray for the momma who wonders why God led her down this path. She can see where she wants to be and what she thought she'd be doing, but her expectations don't match her reality. Lord, help her see the safety of this road. Remind her that she's walking down it because You knew these steps were the best route to her future. She didn't get here by accident. She didn't get here because she made a mistake. You are careful to lead the ones You love, and You love her. Bless her tonight. We ask in Jesus's name. Amen.

Tonight I'm praying this for _____.

October 1

Tonight we pray for the momma whose baby just won't sleep. Lord, this little one has her days and nights mixed up. Or maybe she is experiencing sleep regression and is constantly waking up in the night. There are a myriad of reasons babies just won't sleep during the night; this baby may be teething, sick, colicky, or hungry. Lord, this momma is tired. She is weary to her bones. She needs rest so she can handle all the duties of the day. Help this momma figure out this sleep puzzle. Tonight we ask You to supernaturally multiply what little sleep she does get. Bring her strength for tomorrow. We ask in Jesus's name. Amen.

Tonight I'm praying this for _____.

October 2

*T*onight we pray for the momma who is desperate for a miracle. She needs something to change. Lord, she needs You to step in and do what only You can do. She needs a rescue. Where everything seems hopeless or without an answer, Lord, You are the help in her present time of trouble. We ask that You'd change this situation for her good and for the good of those she loves. You are hope and peace and strength and wisdom and mercy and provision. You are the God who has everything she needs and who doesn't withhold any of it from her. Perform a miracle in her life now. We ask in Jesus's name. Amen.

> God is our refuge and strength,
> an ever-present help in trouble. (Psalm 46:1)

Tonight I'm praying this for _____.

October 3

Tonight we pray for the momma whose spouse has a dangerous occupation. Lord, this job requires hard physical work. Her spouse is often gone for long stretches of time, and she has to run the household all by herself. She may be trying to get used to this life, or she may have been doing this for many years. But it never really gets easier. Lord, we ask that You would watch over her spouse. Help him stay safe on the rig or out on the jobsite. We pray for this momma as she keeps everything moving along at home. Lord, tonight we ask for Your grace and strength to carry her through these days. Give her a good night's rest so tomorrow she can awaken refreshed to start again. We ask in Jesus's name. Amen.

Tonight I'm praying this for _____.

October 4

Tonight we pray for the momma who is the last one awake in her home. Long after her children have gone to sleep, she puts away toys and resets the house for the next day. Sometimes she watches something on television. Sometimes she just scrolls on her phone. Lord, some nights she appreciates the peace and quiet, and other nights she just feels lonely. She'd love to have someone to tell all her feelings to, someone who seems to really care about the weight she carried all day. Lord, she's not as alone as she feels. Tonight You are right there with her, sitting with her, listening to her share her day. And while You already know what happened, You love to hear her share it from her perspective. Help her release the stress, and grant her rest tonight. We ask in Jesus's name. Amen.

Tonight I'm praying this for _____.

October 5

onight we pray for the momma who gets up and just keeps going. She isn't always sure how she's going to find the strength to make it until bedtime, but she always does. She is more amazing than she realizes. She's a warrior. Lord, this momma has another day ahead of her tomorrow, full of responsibilities and obligations that will prevent her from sitting to rest. Tonight we ask that You'd supernaturally multiply her strength. Rise up inside her so that tomorrow as she takes on the day, she will feel Your power propelling her forward. With You as her strength, she cannot fail. Give her peace tonight, and help her sleep. We ask in Jesus's name. Amen.

Tonight I'm praying this for _____.

Tonight we pray for the momma who needs a job, a way to help support her family. Lord, she knows You are her source, but she is trusting You to lead her to an opportunity that is best for her whole family. She is thinking about her family's list of activities and trying to figure out how best to fit in a new work schedule. She is thinking about childcare arrangements and whether her family can help with this. Lord, You already have this momma's new position in mind. Show her whom to call and which doors to knock on. Give her peace as she trusts You with tomorrow. We ask in Jesus's name. Amen.

Tonight I'm praying this for _____.

October 7

onight we pray for the momma who finds even the everyday tasks too difficult because she is so overwhelmed. She sometimes has to work up her courage to go into a store, mail a letter at the post office, return an email, or even make an appointment on the phone. She has to work hard at the simplest things of life that come easily to others. Lord, the deep exhaustion she feels about ordinary tasks depletes her strength for all the fun things in life, such as playing games with her children or doing an art project or a home project. Tonight we ask for healing for this momma. We ask for the right resources to help her overcome her anxiety or depression. We ask especially for Your grace, mercy, and peace to be her portion. We ask in Jesus's name. Amen.

The LORD is my rock and my fortress and my deliverer;
My God, my strength, in whom I will trust;
My shield and the horn of my salvation, my stronghold.
(Psalm 18:2, NKJV)

Tonight I'm praying this for _____.

October 8

Tonight we pray for the momma who is fighting breast cancer. She may have just been diagnosed, or she may be in the middle of the fight for her life. Lord, this can be a scary and stressful time. She may be going through chemotherapy and radiation treatments. She may be trying to decide if she will have a mastectomy or a lumpectomy. The decisions are endless. The fear can be overwhelming. The nights are long and often full of worry. Lord, You are right by her side, holding her close and speaking words of peace and calm. You are the God who heals. Send her to a great medical team. Help her have all the resources she needs for a successful fight. Watch over her family during this difficult time. We ask in Jesus's name. Amen.

Tonight I'm praying this for _____.

Tonight we pray for the momma who is afraid of tomorrow. She can't sleep tonight because she is so fearful of what tomorrow will bring. Lord, please remind her that You hold every tomorrow in Your hands. You have such a beautiful and lovely plan for her life. If it is a specific event she is dreading, please remind her that it is easier to face it in the morning when the sun comes up. Tonight, may she rest in the knowledge that You are working everything out for her benefit and her good. Let her close her eyes knowing that You are watching over every aspect of her future. We ask in Jesus's name. Amen.

Tonight I'm praying this for _____.

October 10

Tonight we pray for the momma who literally never has a day off. She is on duty twenty-four seven. She'd give just about anything for a day when she didn't have to do something. Lord, this momma needs a good break. She needs someone who can come and take over her responsibilities so she can check out and recenter her heart on who You are in her. Lord, this momma's schedule is full, but her heart is fuller. Give her the grace to carry on even when she doesn't know where the strength is going to come from. Restore her heart while she sleeps tonight, God. We ask in Jesus's name. Amen.

Tonight I'm praying this for _____.

October 11

*T*onight we pray for the momma who is struggling with her past. She tries to forget the pain and move on, but sometimes—especially at night—it just creeps up on her heart. Lord, the wounds have healed but the scars remain. Tonight we pray that the memories of past hurts do not steal the joy of today. We ask for more peace for this momma. Help her rest tonight so she may be refreshed in the morning. We ask in Jesus's name. Amen.

Tonight I'm praying this for _____.

Tonight we pray for the momma of the curious toddler. Lord, this little one always seems to be getting into something, and this momma can never turn her back, even for a second. Lord, this momma is tired. She never has a break when she can just relax and trust that everything is going to be okay. She must continually keep her guard up and stay vigilant in paying attention to this little one's every move. We ask that You'd give her rest tonight. Help her remember that this stage won't last forever. They will navigate it together, and You will help them. Bring this momma peace, and remind her that she's doing a good job. We ask in Jesus's name. Amen.

Tonight I'm praying this for _____.

October 13

Tonight we pray for the momma who is in the hospital. Lord, she is away from her children, and she can't stop thinking about them. She is wondering if they are okay, if they had a good dinner, if they are doing their homework. She wonders if they are sad or scared or worried because the routine has been disrupted. Even though she speaks with them on the phone, it is not the same as being home with them and making sure everything is going along as usual. Lord, help this momma rest. Help her heal so she can go home and continue her normal activities. Be with her and her family in this difficult time. We ask in Jesus's name. Amen.

Tonight I'm praying this for _____.

Tonight we pray for the momma of a newborn. She is running on empty. Caring for an infant is harder than she ever imagined. While others tried to help her get ready for this experience, nothing could have prepared her for just how exhausted she would be all the time. Lord, she has a long night ahead of her. She has so many dark hours before the sun rises again. Give her rest tonight. Strengthen her mentally, physically, spiritually, and emotionally. Give her wisdom to know which people to reach out to who can come alongside her and give her help. Bring this momma peace. We ask in Jesus's name. Amen.

Tonight I'm praying this for _____.

October 15

Tonight we pray for the momma who has suffered a miscarriage or stillbirth. Lord, her heart is broken. She had so many hopes and dreams for her baby. She was looking forward to experiencing many firsts with this little one. This season has been filled with countless tears and many sleepless nights. She might feel as though somehow she failed and disappointed many people. Lord, we pray for this momma tonight, and we ask that You would comfort her as only You can. We pray that You would help her heal in both her heart and her body. We trust that You are good even when it seems as if the world has fallen apart. Give this momma rest tonight. We ask in Jesus's name. Amen.

Tonight I'm praying this for _____.

*T*onight we pray for the momma who needs to be seen. Lord, she feels invisible in her life, in her home, and in her career. She needs affirmation that she is valuable as a person, not just a momma. Lord, please be with her and help others see her as You see her. She is uniquely created by You and is so precious. Help her feel Your love surround her tonight. We ask in Jesus's name. Amen.

Tonight I'm praying this for _____.

onight we pray for the momma who feels boxed in by all her responsibilities. Lord, she is a creative person who loves spontaneity, but her life and schedule do not allow it. Tonight, Lord, we ask that You would meet this momma right in the middle of all her busyness and bless her in her creativity. Help her find a time when that wonderful gift can be expressed and nurtured. Lord, please bless her time and multiply it. Help her find those moments that refuel and refresh her so she can be the best momma for her children. We ask in Jesus's name. Amen.

Tonight I'm praying this for _____.

onight we pray for the momma who blames herself. Momma guilt is a real thing, and this momma feels at fault for the big things and the little things that have gone wrong. She carries the weight of the world on her shoulders, and she won't put that weight down. Lord, she has carried some of this for so long that she forgets how heavy a burden she bears. We pray that You would help this momma tonight. You said in Matthew 11:28 to come to You when we are heavy laden. So we ask tonight that this momma would come to You and give You all this blame and guilt so she can live without this heaviness. We ask for peace and rest for her tonight. We ask in Jesus's name. Amen.

Create in me a clean heart, O God,
And renew a steadfast spirit within me. (Psalm 51:10, NKJV)

Tonight I'm praying this for _____.

#MidnightMomDevotional

October 19

Tonight we pray for the momma who is depressed. She doesn't want to admit it, but she hasn't felt like herself for a while. She's afraid of what this might mean. She's afraid that she's never going to feel the way she wants to again. Lord, You haven't left this momma to face these feelings alone. You know we live in a broken world and her feelings are not her fault. Give her courage to tell someone who can help her. Give her strength to reach out to friends and counselors. Give her wisdom to know which professional can help her the most. And encourage her heart tonight as she prepares to make important calls tomorrow. She is worth her own attention. Remind her that her health, including her mental health, should not be put on the back burner. Grant her peace and rest tonight. We ask in Jesus's name. Amen.

Tonight I'm praying this for _____.

October 20

Tonight we pray for the momma who wants her children to have their own relationship with God. They might still be little, and she may be guiding and shaping their understanding. They might be middle schoolers or teenagers. They might be young adults who are questioning what they were taught when they were young. Lord, this momma has modeled what it looks like to trust You in all seasons. She has led her children to Your feet and given them to You. We ask that You'd help her lead them. We ask that You'd continue to show her how to encourage and teach them. Thank You for this momma who knows that leading her children into their own relationship with You is paramount to every other ambition. Thank You for loving her and her children. Help this momma rest as she remembers that You will lead her children just as You have led her. We ask in Jesus's name. Amen.

Tonight I'm praying this for _____.

Tonight we pray for the momma who ran out of gas miles ago. Her life was giving her warning signs that she was low on fuel, but she just kept going. Lord, this momma is running on fumes. Some days she wakes up and has no idea how she's still putting one foot in front of the other. Lord, guide her to Your Word. Remind her that she must stay under the fountain of living water so she can have plenty to pour out on those she loves. Speak hope over her weary heart, and give her Scripture verses to stand on in the days ahead. You are her strength. Help her remember this is true. We ask in Jesus's name. Amen.

Tonight I'm praying this for _____.

Tonight we pray for the momma who is a cancer survivor. Lord, she has survived what was probably one of the scariest times in her whole life. She is ready to move on and begin to plan the future again. She is blessed that there is no evidence of the disease in her body. She is perhaps dealing with scars and reconstruction issues, but that is nothing compared to the life-threatening diagnosis You helped her overcome. Thank You for Your healing grace. Tonight we bless this momma on her journey. We are thankful for her health. We ask for restful and restorative sleep for her. We ask in Jesus's name. Amen.

Tonight I'm praying this for _____.

Tonight we pray for the momma who is weathering the storm. Lord, the wind and waves are relentless, but she is holding firm to her faith. She is trusting in You, Lord, to see her to the other side. She is believing that the words from Mark 4:39, "Peace, be still!" (NKJV), apply to her situation. Tonight, Lord, help this momma rest. No matter the circumstances of this storm, she is holding on and trusting You until the morning light. Remind her that joy comes in the morning. We ask in Jesus's name. Amen.

Tonight I'm praying this for _____.

Tonight we pray for the momma who tried but feels as if she failed. Lord, she really thought it was going to work. She put so much thought and energy into making it the best she could. But she fights the feeling that it wasn't enough. She feels like a failure and is discouraged. Lord, You saw this momma's effort. You saw how much love she poured into the steps she took and the decision she made. She isn't a failure. She isn't the outcome of this event. She is Your daughter, and You are proud of her. Help her recognize her successes, God. Help her see how amazing she really is. Bless her tonight. We ask in Jesus's name. Amen.

Tonight I'm praying this for _____.

Tonight we pray for the momma who has an empty nest, whose children are grown and living on their own. Lord, it doesn't matter if her children are under her roof or live thousands of miles away; she will still pray for them. They are still hers, and she is always concerned with their lives, their health, their future. Tonight, Lord, she brings them to You again. She asks that You would watch over them, keep them safe, and let them fulfill their destinies in You. She prays for their financial well-being, their safety, and their children—her grandchildren. Bless this momma as she continues to pray nightly. We ask in Jesus's name. Amen.

Tonight I'm praying this for _____.

Tonight we pray for the momma who needs to feel loved. Lord, she needs to know that You love her and that her family loves her. Sometimes she feels as though the people closest to her love what she does for them but don't fully love who she is. Lord, remind this momma of Your truth: You sent Your Son to die on the cross just for her. If You could have sent Jesus and gained only her in exchange, You would have because she is valuable to You. Lord, help her family show her this week just how much she means to them. Her worth is found not in what she accomplishes but rather in who she is and who she was created to be. She is Yours, and Your love means the most. Give her sweet sleep tonight. We ask in Jesus's name. Amen.

Tonight I'm praying this for _____.

October 27

Tonight we pray for the weariest of mommas. Lord, she has gone nonstop for what feels like years on end, and though the seasons are changing, her load isn't getting any lighter. She gets the least amount of sleep in her home, and yet it seems as though she does most of the work. Lord, bless this momma with rest tonight. Give her supernatural strength as she sleeps so that no matter how much or how little sleep she gets tonight, she wakes up feeling refreshed. Send Your Holy Spirit to be a healing oil for this momma's heart. Help her feel close to You now—so close that nothing else matters and she knows she can face whatever is ahead with You. We ask in Jesus's name. Amen.

Tonight I'm praying this for _____.

Tonight we pray for the momma who is anxious due to an underlying genetic condition. Lord, she may have a disorder that doesn't allow her to create or process the chemicals she needs for healthy emotional functioning. It is not a sign of weakness when she feels anxious; it is actually a physical condition that affects her mental health. Tonight, Lord, we pray for this momma. We ask that You would heal her all the way down to her genetic code. We know that You are able to heal all our diseases. We thank You for healing this momma. We ask for rest tonight. We ask in Jesus's name. Amen.

Tonight I'm praying this for _____.

Tonight we pray for the momma who is worried about ruining her children. Lord, she worries about what they eat, how much they exercise, whether she is patient enough with them, and whether she is protecting their little hearts from the world. Lord, each of these worries is on her mind tonight. She is thinking back over the day and tallying every place she feels she failed. We ask for Your peace to settle on her heart, wiping the score clean. Reassure her that she is doing her best and that You say she is a good mom. Help her rest tonight. We ask in Jesus's name. Amen.

Tonight I'm praying this for _____.

onight we pray for the momma who makes time for everyone but herself. Maybe it's snuggling with her baby or reading a book to her toddler. Maybe it's working on homework with her grade-schooler or listening to her teenager. Maybe she makes time for her spouse and her house and her community activities. Maybe it's sports or church or a handful of other obligations she has committed herself to. Whatever it is, Lord, this momma makes sure everyone gets what he needs from her. But, Lord, she rarely has a minute alone. She doesn't have anything left at the end of the day just for herself. So we ask that You'd help this momma find time to pay attention to her own needs. Help her find a minute to rest and enjoy something she loves. Bless this momma tonight. We ask in Jesus's name. Amen.

Tonight I'm praying this for _____.

#MidnightMomDevotional

Tonight we pray for the momma who is trying to balance all the events—carnivals, trunk or treats, and neighborhood parties—with a semblance of sanity and at least some control over the sugar consumed. Lord, she may not even want to acknowledge this day because she feels it is inappropriate for her family, or she may be trying to thread the needle between the scary and the fun for children. Lord, this day can be tricky. We ask that You would help this momma tonight as she makes decisions for her children. Let them rest well tonight after all the excitement. We ask in Jesus's name. Amen.

Tonight I'm praying this for _____.

Tonight we pray for the momma who needs to refresh and refuel her heart for the week ahead. Lord, she needs to find space in all the busyness to be still and hear Your thoughts and her own. Tonight she is looking ahead to the week, and she is not sure when she will find a quiet moment. Lord, we ask that You would open up a space for her to be able to take care of her own heart. Please meet her right in the middle of her week that is jam-packed with obligations. Bless her with rest tonight, and meet her in the morning with Your promise of refreshment and renewal. We ask in Jesus's name. Amen.

Tonight I'm praying this for _____.

*T*onight we pray for the momma whose life was just turned upside down. Lord, it may have been a medical diagnosis she was not expecting, a job layoff, or an unforeseen pregnancy. Lord, this new situation has really tossed her world into confusion, but You are the Prince of Peace. You give us peace in every storm. You calm the wind and the waves, and we believe You will calm the heart of this momma. Lord, as she begins to figure out what this next season looks like, we ask that You would guide every decision she makes with Your wisdom and truth. We pray for peace tonight. We ask in Jesus's name. Amen.

Tonight I'm praying this for _____.

Tonight we pray for the momma who has a child in one of the branches of the military. Lord, when our children are grown, we do not stop worrying about them or praying for them. This momma especially knows how to intercede for her child. So many times she has woken up in the night just to pray and found out later that she was praying at just the right moment. She prays for protection, for guidance, and for wisdom, and we pray those same prayers for her tonight. Be with both her and her child, no matter how near or far away. We ask in Jesus's name. Amen.

Tonight I'm praying this for _____.

November 4

*T*onight we pray for the momma who is anticipating the holiday season of Thanksgiving, Christmas, and New Year's. She is already thinking about travel, Christmas gifts, finances, and maybe even the side dishes for Thanksgiving. Lord, this momma has enough on her daily plate without all the added stress of the holidays. She may also have birthdays and anniversaries to celebrate this time of year. Lord, help her enjoy the celebrations. Help her be kind to herself as she takes on all the planning and gift giving and cooking. She knows what she can accomplish. Please remind her to take her own needs into consideration when others ask for more than she is able to give. Help her rest well tonight. We ask in Jesus's name. Amen.

> Do not worry about tomorrow, for tomorrow will worry about itself. Each day has enough trouble of its own.
> (Matthew 6:34)

Tonight I'm praying this for _____.

*T*onight we pray for the momma who didn't have any practice caring for children before she had one of her own. Lord, she wasn't the neighborhood babysitter, and she didn't have younger siblings. She didn't volunteer in the church nursery, and none of her friends have had children yet. Now she has a newborn, and she doesn't feel prepared to raise such a little one. Lord, please remind her that motherhood is one of nature's most instinctive roles. She already loves her baby, and now she is just learning to care for her and watch over her. She is taking it one day at a time. Lord, please bring her the resources she needs to help her feel more comfortable in her new momma role. Help her find a trusted mentor such as her own momma or grandmomma to talk to about her questions. Please multiply her sleep tonight. We ask in Jesus's name. Amen.

Tonight I'm praying this for _____.

*T*onight we pray for the momma who is just going through the motions. Lord, she cannot remember the last time she was fully engaged with her children. She feels emotionally checked out, as if she's on autopilot. Tonight, Lord, we pray for this momma who is so disengaged from her children, her work, her very life. We pray that You would help her find joy again. Help her as she remembers her deeply held relationships with her children, her spouse, and her community. Help her find the spiritual and medical resources she needs to recapture hope. Bless her tonight, and grant her peace. We ask in Jesus's name. Amen.

Tonight I'm praying this for _____.

November 7

*T*onight we pray for the momma who would just like to go out on a girls' night. Lord, it seems as though it has been forever since she spent time with her friends. She would love to go out to dinner or see a funny movie or even spend time at her friend's house just laughing. Lord, during this busy season, please help this momma find time for a moment to herself. Please help her not to feel guilty about it but to really enjoy it. Bless her with rest tonight, and help her enjoy this holiday season. We ask in Jesus's name. Amen.

Tonight I'm praying this for _____.

Tonight we pray for the momma who has served or is serving her country. Lord, we as a nation are so grateful. We pray that You'd protect her and surround her with Your armies of angels. And if she comes back wounded in mind, body, or spirit, we pray for Your healing grace. We pray for all those who have come back physically wounded or with a traumatic brain injury or suffering from PTSD. We ask that You would help them in their recovery and continue to heal every kind of injury. Help them make remarkable progress. Please help this momma rest well tonight, knowing that we support her. We ask in Jesus's name. Amen.

Tonight I'm praying this for _____.

November 9

*T*onight we pray for the momma whose children don't call to check in and say hi. Lord, she loves them and just wants to hear their voices. She worries that she's a bother and feels rejected when they remain silent for so long. She worries about their health and even their whereabouts sometimes. It just hurts her heart when they don't call or answer when she calls them. Lord, You are the mender of broken hearts. You are the healer of relationships. Tonight we pray that You would help this momma establish appropriate boundaries in her relationships with her adult children. Help them work this out together so that hearts won't be wounded or offended. We ask for Your grace over this situation. We ask in Jesus's name. Amen.

Tonight I'm praying this for _____.

November 10

*T*onight we pray for the momma who just needs everything to come into focus. Lord, she feels as though everything is foggy and unclear. She wonders what to do next, how it is all going to be resolved, and where and when she should take the next step. This momma's heart is full of questions, and she trusts that You have all the answers. Help her see where You're leading. Wipe away all the depression, anxiety, or stress that is keeping her thoughts and heart cloudy. Bless her as the answers come and things begin to make sense. Give her rest tonight. We ask in Jesus's name. Amen.

Tonight I'm praying this for _____.

Tonight we pray for the momma whose spouse is deployed. Lord, she has to do many things alone when her spouse is gone. Sometimes it feels like being a single momma. Lord, we are thankful for her family's service. We ask for protection for her spouse. Send Your angels to watch over him every day. We appreciate all this family does for our country. We don't understand everything that goes into being a military momma, but we do know it involves sacrifice, including the possibility of frequent relocations to different areas of the country and even the world. We lift this momma up to You tonight and pray a special blessing for her and her family. We ask in Jesus's name. Amen.

He shall give His angels charge over you,
To keep you in all your ways. (Psalm 91:11, NKJV)

Tonight I'm praying this for _____.

#MidnightMomDevotional

November 12

Tonight we pray for the momma whose day is full as soon as her feet hit the floor in the morning. Lord, no matter what kind of night she had, no matter how many times she was awakened by the baby or a small child, she still has to be ready to go. Her days are scheduled so tightly because of her job, her appointments, and her family that she barely stops to eat lunch and sometimes skips it altogether. Lord, bless this momma tonight with sweet rest. Help her be refreshed and renewed so that in the morning when she hits the ground running, she is ready. Bless her tonight. We ask in Jesus's name. Amen.

Tonight I'm praying this for _____.

*T*onight we pray for the momma who is ready for the tantrums phase to be over. She is ready for this stage to be long behind her. She fights to maintain peace. She works so hard to prevent meltdowns, but sometimes her child just can't help but break down, usually in the most inconvenient situations. Lord, this momma's heart is worn down. She's exhausted. Please give her supernatural patience. Just when she thinks she is at the end of herself, step in and pour out an extra measure of grace on her and her child. You love them both, and You are working to maintain their relationship in the midst of so many big emotions. Help this momma remember that she is doing the best she can and that You are proud of her. We ask in Jesus's name. Amen.

Tonight I'm praying this for _____.

November 14

*T*onight we pray for the momma who feels alone, even in the midst of a crowd. She feels as if she doesn't have even one friend she can rely on. She needs to talk and be in community with others, and she just can't seem to find even one person who truly listens and cares. She has tried so many avenues to build friendships, but she can't seem to connect on a deeper level with other mommas. Lord, Your Word says in Psalm 68:6 that You set the lonely in families. Tonight we are believing that You, Lord, will fulfill this promise for this momma. Help her sleep well tonight. We ask in Jesus's name. Amen.

Tonight I'm praying this for _____.

Tonight we pray for the momma who needs a clear mind in order to make the right decision. Lord, she needs clarity and focus to decide what her next step should be. In so many situations, we have to make decisions and we don't feel prepared or feel as though we have enough information. But the truth is that You are the one who can help us decide correctly. You know every outcome, and we can trust in You. You sent Your Holy Spirit to guide us into all truth. Lord, we thank You for helping us with this process tonight. Bless this momma, and help her sleep well, knowing that You hold everything in Your hands. We ask in Jesus's name. Amen.

Tonight I'm praying this for _____.

#MidnightMomDevotional

November 16

Tonight we pray for the momma who is so worried she can hardly take a deep breath. Lord, it feels as though every muscle in her body is tight. It feels as if every nerve in her body is on fire. She is restless and can't sleep. She needs to close her eyes because she has a lot to do tomorrow, but she can't seem to relax and fall asleep. Tonight, Lord, we pray that You would give this momma so much peace that it floods her heart. Remind her that You are in control of everything and that she can trust in You. We ask in Jesus's name. Amen.

Tonight I'm praying this for _____.

Tonight we pray for the single momma during this hectic holiday season. Lord, there are Thanksgiving dinners and special events to attend at school. There are extra financial demands on an already-thin budget and more stress on an already-threadbare heart. Lord, please give this momma the extra resources and time she needs to accomplish all the things that are in her heart to make this holiday season special for her children. Please help her rest tonight, knowing that You are right there with her each step of the way. We ask in Jesus's name. Amen.

Tonight I'm praying this for _____.

Tonight we pray for the momma who just needs the sun to shine. This season can be so dreary that it makes this momma feel as if the sky will never be blue and the sun will never shine again. Lord, many places already have snow and cold weather. This season of winter has started early, and it's going to be a long one. Lord, we pray for this momma and ask that You would help her find extra joy in the sunshine of family, friends, and loved ones during the holidays. We ask for rest tonight. May her heart be full of Your light. We ask in Jesus's name. Amen.

Tonight I'm praying this for _____.

Tonight we pray for the momma who is on the mission field. This momma was called to this place and has such a heart for these people. Lord, You have knit her heart to theirs. But being here requires many sacrifices. Her extended family may miss her, the financial support has to be raised, and travel may be a challenge. Lord, she honors her calling as a missionary and as a momma. She is leading her family by demonstrating love and compassion to those who need to hear and see the gospel. Lord, bless this momma tonight with resources for this task. Help her as she raises her little ones to know how to serve You in this unique way. Protect her family and watch over each one. We ask in Jesus's name. Amen.

Tonight I'm praying this for _____.

*T*onight we pray for the momma who is ready for a season of joy. She has been in a season of struggle for too long. It seems as if she has fought to keep her head above water, and tonight she is ready to be on dry land. Lord, You promised that our sorrow would endure only for a season and that joy comes in the morning. Tonight we ask that You would bring this momma into a season of joy, peace, and grace. Rescue her from the waves. We ask in Jesus's name. Amen.

Tonight I'm praying this for _____.

November 21

Tonight we pray for the momma who loves and takes care of so many children who aren't her own. Lord, from the neighborhood kids to kids in her church family and from distant relatives to her children's friends, this momma has an eye out and a heart open for everyone. She is a listening ear for those who need it, a hug for others, and a shoulder to cry on for many. Lord, bless this momma. Show her just how many lives she is touching. She doesn't do this just for them; she does this because she knows You love them even more than she does. Give her strength and wisdom to know how to best reach the world around her. Reveal to her just how special she really is. Bring her peace. We ask in Jesus's name. Amen.

Tonight I'm praying this for _____.

*T*onight we pray for the momma who works in the health-care system. She may be a technician, an assistant, a therapist, a radiologist, a nurse, a pharmacist, an intern, a resident, a psychologist, an anesthesiologist, a surgeon, or a doctor, or she may fill another highly important position. Whatever role she plays in this field, it is vital to the functioning of the health-care system. Lord, none of these jobs are easy. They require skill and a specialized education and dedication to the health of others. Bless this momma tonight. In the middle of the cold and flu season, we are so grateful for such a dedicated worker. We ask that You would keep her healthy as she journeys onward in her chosen profession of caring for those who are the sickest. Tonight we pray that You would remind her of how valuable she is. We ask in Jesus's name. Amen.

Tonight I'm praying this for _____.

*T*onight we pray for the momma who is ready to fall into bed but for whom sleep is far away. Lord, she was running all day and never had a chance to sit down and regroup. She rushed from one task or errand to another. She has so many things to do every day in the care and keeping of her house and job. The children take every last ounce of strength—and sometimes even more. Bless her tonight with a good night of sleep so that tomorrow she can awake refreshed and ready to start over. We ask in Jesus's name. Amen.

Tonight I'm praying this for _____.

November 24

*T*onight we pray for the momma whose heart is filled with gratitude for the blessings of this week. Lord, she loves that this week is all about family and relationships. She loves that they will have meaningful conversations around a table full of delicious food. She also knows that this week will involve a lot of work. She is not used to planning a huge meal with unusual side dishes in addition to her weekly routine, but she is up to the task. Lord, bless her this week as she makes a special memory for her family or as she travels to be with family near or far. Continue to fill her heart with gratitude. We ask in Jesus's name. Amen.

Tonight I'm praying this for _____.

*T*onight we pray for the momma who needs an extra measure of grace to deal with her extended family this holiday season. Lord, she loves all of them, but sometimes they may overstep boundaries in the disciplining of her children or in their parenting advice or marital advice or even dating advice. Sometimes, Lord, she has to try hard to keep her composure and continue to be gracious. Lord, You place us in families, and she is thankful for hers. Please remind her that someday she will miss these conversations with her older family members. Help her cherish them today. Encourage this momma's heart as she prepares for the days ahead. We ask in Jesus's name. Amen.

Tonight I'm praying this for _____.

*T*onight we pray for the momma who has traveled to a relative's house for Thanksgiving. Lord, it may be by car or plane, and she has little ones in tow. The challenges of traveling have been made greater by the large number of travelers during this busiest of weekends. Lord, You know every obstacle she has faced. You know every road hazard or plane delay or simple frustration she has endured this week. We ask now that You would smooth the road ahead. We are grateful for family and friends. We ask that You would bless them tonight. We ask in Jesus's name. Amen.

Tonight I'm praying this for _____.

November 27

Tonight we pray for the momma who woke up strong and was able to get so much accomplished today. Lord, it was a good day for her and her family. She may have completed errands or gone to work and finished a project. Perhaps the homeschooling went great. Whatever it was, it was a big success. Lord, we are grateful for the good days, and we thank You for walking with us through the difficult ones. Be with this momma tonight as she rests and gears up for the exciting and hectic month of December and all the joy and obligations it often brings. We pray for Your blessings on her family. We ask Jesus's name. Amen.

Tonight I'm praying this for _____.

Tonight we pray for the momma who is afraid. Lord, she is afraid that things are not going to turn out well. She is afraid that if she lets go and doesn't try to control the situation, something terrible will happen and she will feel as if it's her fault. She wants to be sure everyone is safe. She is fiercely protective, but sometimes trying to control things that are out of her control makes her afraid. Lord, Your Word says in 2 Timothy 1:7 that You did not give us "a spirit of fear, but of power and of love and of a sound mind" (NKJV). Tonight we ask that this momma would trust in You. Please help her turn every situation over to You because she certainly can't control it herself. Bless her with rest tonight. We ask in Jesus's name. Amen.

Tonight I'm praying this for _____.

*T*onight we pray for the momma who has a wonderful extended family who helps her during the holidays. Lord, she reaches out to them for support, and they are always right there with a helping hand. Sometimes they cover for her at a school event when she is stuck at work. They often help with childcare, and they invite her family to share a meal with them as often as they are able. She is grateful for this because she knows not all families do this. Lord, as she names them one by one for a blessing tonight, remind her that You will bless them abundantly. We ask in Jesus's name. Amen.

Tonight I'm praying this for _____.

November 30

*T*onight we pray for the momma of teenagers. Lord, she feels as though she doesn't have the influence she once had when her children were younger. They are part of a social sphere that is beyond her control. Lord, this can be such a stressful time for this momma. She doesn't want to alienate her teens by being intrusive, but teenagers are not able to make all the choices on their own as adults can. Help this momma tonight. Grant her Your wisdom. Grant her heart peace in this difficult season. Be with her children as they transition into adults. We ask in Jesus's name. Amen.

Tonight I'm praying this for _____.

December 1

*T*onight we pray for the momma who is entering this holiday season focused on the Prince of Peace. She remembers that He came so that she could have peace in her heart all year long. Now, Lord, as the holiday festivities begin, full of school Christmas plays and parties and shopping and meals, help her keep her eyes on You. You are the reason we celebrate these festive days. Walk with her, and give her Your rest when she needs it most. We ask in Jesus's name. Amen.

Tonight I'm praying this for _____.

December 2

Tonight we pray for the momma who wants to be generous this holiday season. She wants to open her heart and her home. She wants to make room, but everything feels stretched thin. From her budget to her time, she just feels as if she doesn't have much margin to be as generous as she'd like. Lord, thank You for this momma's heart. Thank You that she looks around and wonders if there's room in her life to make space for others. This momma is a precious part of Your kingdom, and You see her beautiful heart. Show her ways that she can be light and a gift this season. You are so proud of her. Bless her tonight. We ask in Jesus's name. Amen.

Tonight I'm praying this for _____.

December 3

*T*onight we pray for the momma who is far from family this holiday season. Lord, she has people around her who love her, but it's not the same as being with those who know her best. Maybe she is far from her parents or siblings. Maybe she is deployed and far from her children and husband. Maybe she or others in her family moved across the country and she's just missing everyone so much. Lord, You know how she feels. You understand what it is like to be separated from the ones You love. Hold her close right now. Help her find joy despite the distance. Give her opportunities to show her family members just how much they mean to her, and help her feel loved even miles away. We ask in Jesus's name. Amen.

Tonight I'm praying this for _____.

December 4

Tonight we pray for the momma who just wants to sleep. Lord, it's as simple as that request. She is weary, and her greatest prayer is for a full night of uninterrupted sleep. Tonight we ask that You would grant this momma's simple desire for rest. Lord, please make a way for that to happen. Let this momma ask for the help from her family or friends that she so desperately needs, and supernaturally multiply any sleep she gets. We ask in Jesus's name. Amen.

Come to me, all you who are weary and burdened, and
I will give you rest. (Matthew 11:28)

Tonight I'm praying this for _____.

December 5

*T*onight we pray for the momma who has a newborn. Lord, the exhaustion of having such a little one during the holidays means that nothing about the season is the same. Her heart is full, but she feels unsettled because everything is so different this year. Traveling is harder, as is putting up the decorations or baking Christmas treats. It all just feels overwhelming. Lord, tonight help her be able to sleep. Help her remember that Mary had a newborn baby and that this whole season is based on that fact. Multiply this momma's rest tonight. We ask in Jesus's name. Amen.

Tonight I'm praying this for _____.

#MidnightMomDevotional

December 6

Tonight we pray for the momma who wants her heart to feel as clean as the fresh snow that falls during the night in winter. Lord, she wants to have all the sin and shame of her past just washed away so that her heart glistens with Your love. Lord, tonight You want this daughter to receive Your greatest gift, the gift of forgiveness, and to be made whole. Your Word says, "Though your sins are like scarlet, they shall be as white as snow" (Isaiah 1:18). We pray that this momma accepts the gift of Your Son, Jesus, and His sacrifice that we will remember in just a few months at Easter. The precious manger scene leads us all to the Cross and the Resurrection from the tomb so that we may have eternal life and hearts that are as white as Christmas snow. Bless this momma tonight as she makes this decision or renews this consecration. We ask in Jesus's name. Amen.

Tonight I'm praying this for _____.

*T*onight we pray for the momma who has birthdays, anniversaries, and weddings to celebrate in addition to her holiday plans this month. Lord, her money, time, and energy already feel stretched thin. She loves her family and friends and wants to celebrate with each of them, but her calendar is full to overflowing. Tonight, Lord, we ask that You would help this momma not to feel guilty as she makes decisions about what she can and cannot do this month. Lord, You know her heart and her kindness. You know her circumstances. We ask that You'd grant her sweet rest tonight so that in the morning she may wake refreshed and ready for the new day. We ask in Jesus's name. Amen.

Tonight I'm praying this for _____.

December 8

*T*onight we pray for the momma who is in recovery. She has been clean and sober for a period of time, and she wants to keep it that way. Lord, the temptations are many, but she is holding tightly to the hem of Your garment. She is holding on to prayer and to her accountability partner and other forms of support. She is clinging desperately to You. Help her remember to pray as You taught Your disciples: "Lead us not into temptation, but deliver us from the evil one" (Matthew 6:13). Lord, we ask that You would remind this momma that You are walking with her every step of the way. Give her rest tonight. We ask in Jesus's name. Amen.

Tonight I'm praying this for _____.

Tonight we pray for the momma who hopes her family's love for the Lord shines brightly this holiday season. Lord, a myriad of distractions consume our hearts, time, and money. But as her family points to You, Lord, may You lead others to a deeper knowledge of who You are and why You came. Give this momma opportunities to lead others to see You, who came to change everything. Fill her with joy in the midst of this busy time. We ask in Jesus's name. Amen.

Tonight I'm praying this for _____.

December 10

Tonight we pray for the momma who is remembering Christmases past as she hangs up her decorations. Lord, she is remembering loved ones who have gone on or the days when the children were little and gave her handmade ornaments as gifts. She may have an heirloom piece that is used only on the Christmas table, or she may have pictures of the kids with Santa that are put on the mantle. Lord, it is easy to feel nostalgic and almost sad for the days gone by during this time of year. Help this momma's heart find joy in the memories while making new ones right now. Bless her with rest tonight. We ask in Jesus's name. Amen.

Tonight I'm praying this for _____.

December 11

Tonight we pray for the momma of a grown child with financial issues. Lord, she has given so much money to this child that she has put her own finances and well-being in jeopardy. During the holidays, it is especially hard for her to say no when asked. It is easy for her to feel as if she is failing not just her child but her grandchildren as well. Tonight we ask that You would give this momma wisdom. We ask that You would help her find the resources she needs to teach her grown child how to manage money, how to budget, and how to trust You for all things. Give her confidence in her decisions, and surround her heart with peace. We ask in Jesus's name. Amen.

Tonight I'm praying this for _____.

#MidnightMomDevotional

December 12

*T*onight we pray for the momma who is in transition this holiday season. Lord, it may be a relocation, a new job, or a new house. She may be staying with family or friends while everything is being prepared for the next step. Lord, it is so hard to be in transition during the holidays. This is the time when we want all our familiar things around us. It is the time when we feel the closest connection to our past and when we are adding new memories for the future. Lord, help this momma during this season in her family's life. Help her enjoy the adventure of this moment. Let it become a treasured family story. Help her rest tonight. We ask in Jesus's name. Amen.

Tonight I'm praying this for _____.

Tonight we pray for the momma who needs to dream again. Lord, the dreams she had fell to the ground, and she has not been able to pick them back up for some reason. She feels as if the path to her long-held dreams is blocked or maybe was even destroyed by events that were out of her control. But, Lord, You place dreams in our hearts. You give us things to strive for, to work for, and to hope for in this life. Now we pray that You would give this momma a new dream. Help her see it in her heart and run toward it with everything she has. Let this new dream grow and blossom and bring forth new life. We ask in Jesus's name. Amen.

Tonight I'm praying this for _____.

December 14

*T*onight we pray for the momma who is feeling overwhelmed with all the planning, purchasing, wrapping, traveling, and celebrations. Lord, she may be an introvert, or she may just be shy. No matter why she feels this way, the obligation to attend so many gatherings is starting to put a strain on her. Lord, tonight we pray that this momma would remember that she is important during the holidays too. Please let her reach out for the help she needs if things get to be too much. Help her speak up instead of struggling through in silent suffering. Lord, please remind her how much You love her and how important she is to everyone around her. We ask in Jesus's name. Amen.

Tonight I'm praying this for _____.

December 15

*T*onight, Lord, we pray for the momma who has strained family relationships. Lord, there are so many dynamics involved in every family, and it seems some personalities just don't get along. Add to that a family meal during a stressful holiday season, sometimes in a small space, and those interactions can become heated fairly quickly. Lord, You ask us to forgive, and Your Word teaches us in Matthew 18 to forgive seventy times seven. This momma is going to need Your help to get through this with her family. Lord, we pray that this year will be different. We ask for reconciliation and peace for everyone involved. We ask in Jesus's name. Amen.

Tonight I'm praying this for _____.

December 16

Tonight we pray for the momma who is a volunteer in her local community. Lord, she sets an example for her children by giving her time to causes she believes in. She becomes Your hands and feet as she does some of the hard things her community needs. She does not do this for recognition, but she does want her children to watch and see that giving is an important part of living a life of faith. Lord, please bless this momma as she fits this extra joy of volunteering into her hectic holiday schedule. Please help her rest well tonight so she will have strength for tomorrow. We ask in Jesus's name. Amen.

Tonight I'm praying this for _____.

December 17

*T*onight we pray for the momma who needs joy to return to her life. Motherhood has its moments of delight, but so often she feels rushed through life and unable to slow down and savor moments of happiness. Lord, Your Word says, "The joy of the LORD is your strength" (Nehemiah 8:10). It's not her joy or happiness that will fill her heart's cup to overflowing; it's Your joy that will be her source of strength. Tonight, Lord, we ask that You would restore her joy. Heal her heart of all hurts and wounds and trauma so that she might laugh again. Give her hope for tomorrow, God. We ask in Jesus's name. Amen.

Tonight I'm praying this for _____.

December 18

Tonight we pray for the momma who works at a school as a paraprofessional, secretary, counselor, custodian, substitute teacher, cafeteria worker, bus driver, school nurse, principal, crossing guard, playground attendant, or in any other role that contributes to the success of the children's education. Lord, she is ready for the break from school so she can focus on her own family. She is just as excited for Christmas vacation as the teachers and children are. She is looking forward to baking cookies, seeing a Christmas movie, or even just sleeping past 5:00 a.m. Lord, help her be joyous this holiday season, and help her recharge and be ready for when the school bell rings again. We ask in Jesus's name. Amen.

Tonight I'm praying this for _____.

December 19

Tonight we pray for the momma who has a sick child during the holidays. Lord, no matter what else is demanding her time and attention, she has to put a pause on it all because her child takes precedence over everything else. Lord, tonight we pray for Your healing grace for this little one. Whatever is causing the illness—a fever, an upset tummy, chest congestion, or something else—help this momma's baby return to health. Lord, help this momma find rest while she watches over her child. Help the doctors who are caring for this family. We ask in Jesus's name. Amen.

Tonight I'm praying this for _____.

December 20

onight we pray for the momma who lost a loved one this past year. It may have been a parent, a grandparent, a spouse, a child, or a friend. Lord, whoever that special person was, this year has been hard for this momma. Now she is trying to walk the tightrope of joy and sorrow during this holiday season. She knows no holiday will ever be the same. She might be in the early stages of grief, or she might be getting to the place where she can smile at the memories. But no matter where she is, the first Christmas is hard. Lord, we pray tonight that You would comfort her heart as only You can. Please help her be kind to herself as she works her way through this month. Let those who are important to her reach out with understanding. Bless her tonight, and let her heart rest and heal. We ask in Jesus's name. Amen.

> He heals the brokenhearted
> and binds up their wounds. (Psalm 147:3)

Tonight I'm praying this for _____.

December 21

Tonight we pray for the momma whose child will spend part of the holiday season away from her. Lord, it might be the first year or the tenth, but it is still hard to let her child go during this season. She knows he will be loved and cared for and cherished, but her heart will be missing a piece until he returns. Lord, help this momma rest. Bless her and her child with peace tonight. We ask in Jesus's name. Amen.

Tonight I'm praying this for _____.

December 22

Tonight we pray for the momma who is thinking, *I'm nearing the finish line.* Lord, she is almost ready for the holidays, and she is counting down the hours until Christmas Eve. Tonight we ask that You would let her find joy in this holiday in new and special ways. We pray for amazing surprises this season; may unexpected blessings overflow her cup of joy. Bless this momma who has worked hard to make this day special for those she loves and those in her community. Please give her rest tonight. We ask in Jesus's name. Amen.

Tonight I'm praying this for _____.

Tonight we pray for the momma who is looking forward to the next few days with joy, hope, peace, and excitement. Lord, she has worked hard to get everything ready. She has decorated her tree and her house and may have packed her family's bags for travel. She has bought the presents and either gathered the ingredients for Christmas dinner or ordered a premade meal if that's what her situation this year called for. No matter how she has prepared, she is ready and is anticipating a wonderful time with her family or friends. Bless this momma tonight. We ask in Jesus's name. Amen.

Tonight I'm praying this for _____.

December 24

*T*onight, on this most special night, we pray for the momma who is still awake long after her family has gone to sleep. She may be up wrapping presents, putting the finishing touches on Christmas dinner preparations, or getting ready to travel to see relatives. There is so much to do at Christmas when you're the momma, and she just wants her family to be happy tomorrow. She can't wait to see the look in the eyes of her precious little ones when they see their presents. Deep in her heart she hopes that her preparations have been enough to make the ones she loves know that they are precious to her. Remind her tonight that You are the love we feel during this season and that her efforts are more than enough. Bless this momma with Christmas joy tonight as she celebrates Your birth in Bethlehem. We ask in Jesus's name. Amen.

Tonight I'm praying this for _____.

*T*onight we pray for the momma who is thankful for the gift of Your Son, Jesus, and the peace that He brings to her family. Like so many birthdays, Jesus's birthday is full of preparation for those who celebrate. This momma might have put up decorations and made special foods and done all she could to make this year memorable for those she loves. As the day comes to a close, she's thinking about cleaning up and maybe traveling home by car or plane. Tonight, Lord, help this momma keep the joy of this day in her heart and home a little longer. Help her continue to focus on the wonder of Jesus's birth and what He means to us every day of the year. Tonight we ask for a special Christmas blessing for this momma and her family. We ask in Jesus's name. Amen.

Tonight I'm praying this for _____.

December 26

Tonight we pray for the momma who is wondering how the kids can be bored. Lord, it makes her heart sad when they fuss or complain the day after Christmas. They have so many new things to enjoy and play with, either alone or together, but somehow they manage to argue with one another about pretty much everything. Lord, tonight everyone just needs a minute to regroup and return to a normal schedule and sleeping routine. Bless this momma as she tries to right this ship that seems to have capsized under the weight of the holiday. Help her rest and regain her strength for tomorrow. We ask in Jesus's name. Amen.

Tonight I'm praying this for _____.

December 27

Tonight we pray for the momma who wishes she had kept better records, taken more pictures, or written down important dates. Lord, she experienced all these special times with her children, but sometimes she regrets not pausing to document more. Lord, stir up the memories of all the precious times she doesn't want to forget. Help her find a moment to make a note of them in her journal. Her memories are such a gift in this season of motherhood. Help her extend grace to herself and cherish the moments that were all too fleeting. She's a good momma, and her children will remember all the ways she demonstrated her love. Help her rest in this truth. We ask in Jesus's name. Amen.

Tonight I'm praying this for _____.

December 28

*T*onight we pray for the momma who is ready for the fresh start that the new year brings. Lord, she is ready to turn the page on this past year and begin the new challenges of the next year. There are many changes she hopes to make in the new year, such as better health, more time with family, and more time in prayer and Your Word, but mostly she is looking for fresh hope. Lord, she doesn't have to wait for the new year to receive that gift. Please fill her heart with fresh hope this week. Please, Lord, bless this momma with rest tonight. We ask in Jesus's name. Amen.

Tonight I'm praying this for _____.

*T*onight we pray for the momma who feels as though she does everything differently than everyone else. Lord, whether it's the way she approaches her children's schooling or the way she does her hair, she seems to be marching to the beat of her own drum. Lord, this momma is unique and beautiful. You hear such a sweet song from her life. She doesn't blend in because You made her an individual melody. Help her see the beauty of doing things her own way. She is so precious to You. Give her peace and confidence in who You made her to be. We ask in Jesus's name. Amen.

Tonight I'm praying this for _____.

December 30

onight we pray for the momma who loves her family with her whole heart. Lord, they are her focus. She plans her days around what is best for them. If she has to work, she takes a job that is the best fit for her family, not necessarily the best fit for her hopes and dreams. She thinks about her family before she purchases anything for herself. She measures her time by how much of it she will be able to give to them. Lord, as she prepares for the new year, many would say she should focus more on herself. But she is focusing on herself by doing what makes her happiest, and that is caring for her family. Lord, bless her tonight, and give her rest and peace for this upcoming year. We ask in Jesus's name. Amen.

Tonight I'm praying this for _____.

Tonight we pray for the momma who is looking forward to the new year with hope and anticipation. Lord, she is staying up until midnight to celebrate with joy the start of the new year, the start of something fresh, a clean slate to write her hopes and dreams on. Lord, You are the one who gives us hope. We pray that the excitement she feels and the anticipation of new beginnings will carry over for weeks to come. Meet her with breakthrough in areas where she needs Your power this year. Meet her with hope in areas where she previously felt hopeless. Meet her with strength and expectation and love. Bless this momma and her dreams tonight. We ask in Jesus's name. Amen.

Tonight I'm praying this for _____.

#MidnightMomDevotional

Index

Y

Encouragement for a Momma's Heart

www.BeckyThompson.com

 WATERBROOK